Living
in the
Abundance
of God

WITH COMMENTARY AND A FOREWORD FROM

Joel Osteen

Living
in the
Abundance
of God

JOHN OSTEEN

Faith
Words

New York | Boston | Nashville

Unless otherwise indicated, Scriptures are taken from the *New King James Version.* Copyright © 1979, 1980, 1982, Thomas Nelson, Inc., Publishers. All rights reserved.

Scriptures noted AMP are taken from the *Amplified® Bible.* Copyright © 1954, 1962, 1965, 1987 by The Lockman Foundation. Used by permission.

Literary development and design: Koechel Peterson & Associates, Inc., Mpls., MN.

FaithWords
Hachette Book Group
237 Park Avenue
New York, NY 10017
www.faithwords.com

Printed in the United States of America

First Edition: May 2013
10 9 8 7 6 5 4 3 2 1

FaithWords is a division of Hachette Book Group, Inc.
The FaithWords name and logo are trademarks of Hachette Book Group, Inc.

The Hachette Speakers Bureau provides a wide range of authors for speaking events. To find out more, go to www.hachettespeakersbureau.com or call (866) 376-6591.

The publisher is not responsible for websites (or their content) that are not owned by the publisher.

ISBN: 978-0-89296-885-5

Library of Congress Control Number: 2013930908

Foreword by Joel Osteen

MY DAD WAS RAISED in an extremely poor family, losing everything they owned during the Great Depression. As was true of most people of that generation, he grew up with a "poverty mentality" that shaped his formative years and, as you'll read in this book, had a big influence on his Christian life as well as his ministry. When God tried to bless and increase my dad, he couldn't receive the abundance of God at first. In fact, for many years he thought he was doing God a favor by staying poor. Later, Daddy learned that as God's children, we are able to live an abundant life; that we should even expect to be blessed. Indeed, it is as important to learn how to receive a blessing as it is to be willing to give one.

When God led the Hebrew people out of slavery in Egypt, the eleven-day journey to the Promised Land took forty years. God wanted them to move forward, but they wandered in the desert, going around the same mountain, time after time. They were trapped in a poor, defeated mentality, focusing on their problems and always complaining about the obstacles.

Because of their disobedience and lack of faith, the Israelites spent forty years wandering around in the wilderness. How sad! God had prepared a place of tremendous abundance, a place of great freedom for His people. But their oppressors had beaten them down for so long—mistreated and taken advantage of them—now, even though God wanted a better life for each of them, they couldn't conceive it.

Do you feel as though you're spinning your wheels in life? Rather than moving forward with an attitude of faith, expecting good things, are you allowing obstacles to stand between you and your destiny?

If you listen closely, I believe you'll hear God saying what He said to the Israelites, "You have dwelt long enough on this mountain. . . . Behold, I have set the land before you; go in and take possession of the land which the Lord swore to your fathers . . . to give to them and to their descendants after them" (Deuteronomy 1:6, 8 AMP). No matter what you've gone through in the past, no matter how many setbacks you've suffered or who or what has tried to thwart your progress, today is a new day, and God wants to do a new thing in your life. Don't let your past determine your future.

My dad said that from the moment he gave his heart to Christ at the age of seventeen, "I made a quality decision that my children and family would never have to experience the lack that I was raised in." He searched the Scriptures to see what God said about him and started seeing himself not as a farmer's child with no future but as a child of the Most High God. He rose up and broke the curse of poverty in our family and eventually discovered what it means to live in the abundance of God—spiritually, mentally, and physically.

In Jeremiah 29:11, the Lord declares, "For I know the thoughts that I think toward you, . . . thoughts of peace and not of evil, to give you a future and a hope." It's time to let go of past hurts, pains, or failures. It is time to stretch your faith and pursue the excellence that God has placed in your heart. It is time to break out of the "barely get by" mentality, to become the best you can be, not merely average or ordinary, for the rest of your life. Refuse to be counted among the doubters.

Are you allowing obstacles to stand between you and your destiny?

Friend, I trust that this book will help lead you to break through the barriers of your past and enter into the abundant life God has for you today. We serve the Most High God, and His dream for your life is so much bigger and better than you can even imagine. Never settle for a small view of God. Start thinking as God thinks. Think big. Think increase. Think abundance. Think more than enough!

I think you'll see from the commentary I have added at the end of every chapter that I can't agree more with my father's belief that you can start to enjoy a new life filled with abundance as you are transformed and renewed by God's Word. No matter where you are or what challenges you face, if you dare to believe God and just act on His Word, the possibilities are endless!

"FOR I KNOW THE THOUGHTS

THAT I THINK TOWARD YOU,

. . . THOUGHTS OF PEACE

AND NOT OF EVIL,

TO GIVE YOU A FUTURE AND A HOPE."

JEREMIAH 29:1

Introduction

I love people and desire to help everyone find the best for their life. The Lord God desires to pour out the abundance of His love and mercy and power upon us, but far too often we fail to recognize His presence and guidance when it comes. The Lord is so near, and every one of the promises He has made in His Word for us are true, yet we do not recognize it. If we will only believe that all things are possible to those who believe what He has said and done and provides, it will change our lives.

The Bible states that Jesus is the King of kings and the Lord of lords. Have you ever wondered who the other kings and lords are? Well, you may not feel like one, but you became one of them the moment you received Jesus Christ as your Savior. God's intention is that every believer would reign as a king in this life through Jesus Christ.

CREATED TO BE KINGS

Consider this bedrock truth that God created us to be kings and priests: "From Jesus Christ, the faithful witness, the firstborn from the dead, and the ruler over the kings of the earth. To Him who loved us and washed us from our sins in His own blood, and has made us kings and priests to His God and Father, to Him be glory and dominion forever and ever. Amen" (Revelation 1:5–6).

Why is it that we readily accept the truth that Jesus is the King of kings and Lord of lords, but we hesitate when it comes to the truth of who we are? God says that because He loved us and washed away our sins in His blood, we are to live in His abundance as kings and priests. That is marvelous Good News, yet this is what I hear so many believers say: "Let's just hold out to the end. We may barely make it through this life. We may get to heaven dressed in rags, but in the next life we will reign."

That is certainly not what the apostle Paul tells us in Romans 5:17: "For if by the one man's offense death reigned through the one, much more those who receive abundance of grace and of the gift of righteousness will reign in life through the One, Jesus Christ." Yes, death reigned in life through the sin of Adam, but we who have received the abundance of grace and the gift of right-eousness are to reign in life through Jesus Christ!

In the midst of trials,
in the midst of tribulations,
in the midst of the uncertainties of life,
in the midst of raising a family,
in the midst of all the problems that are hurled at us,
we are to live independent of circumstances
in the abundance of God and reign as kings!

You may say:
"I don't see it!"
You will.
"I can't do it!"
You will.
"I don't understand it!"
You will soon.
"I feel like a slave!"
You will feel differently.

God has given you this book so that you can learn to live in the abundance of God and reign victoriously as a king over your circumstances even . . .

in the midst of a broken home,
in the midst of divorce,
in the midst of the disappointments of life.

TO REIGN IN LIFE IS TO LIVE IN GOD'S ABUNDANCE

Read Romans 5:17 again. "For if by the one man's offense death reigned through the one, much more those who receive abundance of grace and of the gift of righteousness will reign in life through the One, Jesus Christ."

God has given us three profound truths in this single verse. *First, it is possible to receive the abundance of God and to reign in this life.* If we are not reigning in some areas, we are missing out on God's best. And make no mistake about it, whatever comes against us to defeat us from reigning is not God's will.

Second, we are to reign in life through the One, Jesus Christ. We cannot reign as kings in our own power. We must be one with Christ. Since we reign by One, we only need to be concerned about our relationship with Him. He makes it possible for each of us to reign.

Third, we reign in life because we have received the abundance of God's grace and the gift of Jesus' righteousness. If we do not understand grace and righteousness, we will live under condemnation all our lives. To reign as kings we must understand that we have received salvation through the abundant grace of God and not through our own works. "For by grace you have been saved through faith, and that not of yourselves; it is the gift of God, not of works, lest anyone should boast" (Ephesians 2:8–9). And in the eyes of our heavenly Father, we are as righteous as the Lord Jesus Christ (2 Corinthians 5:21). We are the righteousness of God. Therefore, we will reign in this life as kings.

> *We are to reign as kings over . . .*
> *our bodies,*
> *our carnal minds,*
> *our homes,*
> *our circumstances,*
> *every power of darkness,*
> *and every sickness and disease.*

OUR SPIRITUAL HERITAGE IN CHRIST

This truth of living in the abundance of God is based on the fact that we have been made kings and lords of all by the great love of God. "The Spirit Himself bears witness with our spirit that we are children of God, and if children, then heirs—heirs of God and joint heirs with Christ, if indeed we suffer with Him, that we may also be glorified together" (Romans 8:16–17). We are heirs of God, joint heirs with Jesus.

There are three things that will keep us from knowing that we are lords of all—laziness, indifference, and a pre-occupation with the world. If you continue as a child in your thinking, if you are uninformed in your spirit, if you are lazy and indifferent, if you are preoccupied with the things of this world, you will live as a slave to sin and self and not function as a king in this life.

Why do we have the Holy Spirit living within us? "Now we have received, not the spirit of the world, but the Spirit who is from God, that we might know the things that have been freely given to us by God" (1 Corinthians 2:12). The Holy Spirit dwells within us that we may understand the things that God has freely given to us. He wants to teach us the truths of the Word of God so that Satan will not be able to rob us of the blessings and abundance God has for us in this life. The Holy Spirit desires that we might fully know what God has provided for us.

When you are born into the family of God through the Holy Spirit, you are like a newborn baby. You have no spiritual past. Your sins and failures are gone and not remembered. You are a new creature in Christ Jesus. There is no past with God. Forget yesterday, and the yesterday before that! Forget it! God has wiped it away!

First Corinthians 3:1–3 tells that there are three kinds of Christians: "And I, brethren, could not speak to you as to *spiritual* people but as to *carnal*, as to *babes* in Christ. I fed you with milk and not with solid food; for until now you were not able to receive it, and even now you are still not able; for you are still carnal. For where there are envy, strife, and divisions among you, are you not carnal and behaving like mere men?"

There are newborn Christians who need gentle care and to be fed with "milk," the basic truths of God's Word. A new Christian is often carnal, because he has not yet learned many truths from the Word of God. Carnal Christians walk as men and women who are not ruled by the Spirit of God, whereas spiritual Christians are.

Many believers are involved in questionable activities that keep them in a worldly or carnal state. If we only knew the power of looking at something with our eyes or hearing something with our ears, registering that with our brains, and sending it down to our spirits, we would be more careful to guard our eyes and our ears. Far too many believers remain trapped in a life of constant carnality, which in the Corinthians' situation manifested itself in envy, strife, and divisions, because they were still slaves of sin.

It Is Time to Move Into the Abundance of God

All kinds of blessings are available to those Christians who walk after the Spirit of God and not after the flesh.

A close friend shared with me a dream that the Lord had given her in the night. This dream came at a time when her family had great needs. They had not yet come to understand how to reign in life through Jesus Christ. God revealed to her the most lovely banquet table, exquisitely set and filled with beautiful food. She watched herself sit down at her place, surrounded by such abundance, then she reached around all that luscious food, pulled out a dry peanut butter and jelly sandwich, and proceeded to eat it. Then God gave her an understanding of that dream.

He had provided far more for her family than they were taking. Now, she and her husband have learned how to reign as kings.

It is time to move into the abundance of God. Jesus came and completed His redemptive work on the cross and has sat down at the right hand of the throne of God. This is the age of the Holy Spirit. We are living in the day that God spoke of through the prophet Joel when He said, "And it shall come to pass afterward that I will pour out My Spirit on all flesh; your sons and your daughters shall prophesy, your old men shall dream dreams, your young men shall see visions. And also on My menservants and on My maidservants I will pour out My Spirit in those days" (Joel 2:28–29).

The prophet Ezekiel saw the throne of God in the great house of God. Out from the throne of God flowed a river of life to touch the world. "Then he brought me back to the door of the temple; and there was water, flowing from under the threshold of the temple toward the east . . . And when the man went out to the east with the line in his hand, he measured one thousand cubits, and he brought me through the waters; the water came up to my ankles. Again he measured one thousand and brought me through the waters; the water came up to my knees. Again he measured one thousand and brought me through; the water came up to my waist. Again he measured one thousand, and it was a river that I could not cross; for the water was too deep, water in which one must swim, a river that could not be crossed. . . . Then he said to me: 'This water flows toward the eastern region, goes down into the valley, and enters the sea. When it reaches the sea, its waters are healed. And it shall be that every living thing that moves, wherever the rivers go, will live. There will be a very great multitude of fish, because these waters go there; *for they will be healed, and everything will live wherever the river goes*'" (Ezekiel 47:1–9).

This is the mighty river of God's Spirit that flows out to the world through His people. God never started a church denomination. God started a river of people flowing out from the house of God to a needy world. They were to flow out to the world to help and to heal humanity through the power of the Holy Spirit.

This is the age
of the Holy Spirit.

Jesus said, "The Spirit of the LORD is upon Me, because He has anointed Me to preach the gospel to the poor; He has sent Me to heal the brokenhearted, to proclaim liberty to the captives and recovery of sight to the blind, to set at liberty those who are oppressed" (Luke 4:18).

Jesus told the disciples that when He had ascended to heaven they would know that He had made it back, because He would send the blessed Holy Spirit (John 16:7). One hundred and twenty people gather in the upper room in Jerusalem as Jesus commanded (Luke 24:49), where He said, "You shall receive power when the Holy Spirit has come upon you" (Acts 1:8). And the Bible adds, "When the Day of Pentecost had fully come, they were all with one accord in one place. And suddenly there came a sound from heaven, as of a rushing mighty wind, and it filled the whole house where they were sitting. Then there appeared to them divided tongues, as of fire, and one sat upon each of them. And they were all filled with the Holy Spirit and began to speak with other tongues, as the Spirit gave them utterance" (Acts 2:1–4).

Pentecost was the fulfillment of the prophecy of Joel and the beginning of that river flowing out from the throne of God as prophesied by Ezekiel. Continue to read in the book of Acts and you'll see that the river of the Spirit of God began to flow out to this darkened world in tremendous power. In Acts 2, Peter's first sermon was so powerful that 3,000 people were brought to faith and baptized as a result. In Acts 3, we see the rivers of healing power flowing from the throne of God, through the believers to touch a crippled man and completely restore his health. In Acts 4, persecution arose against the church, but rivers of unity bound the Spirit-filled believers together as one. God's people in the book of Acts risked their lives in order to flow like a mighty river to a world in need.

Come Into the Deep Waters

This powerful river of God's Spirit will never be bound by denominational creeds and doctrines. Walls cannot contain it. God is going to let the river rise until we all flow together throughout the world. We will bear one Name. That is the Name that is above every other name. It is the Name of Jesus!

Look at the river of people flowing out from the throne of God. It is a river of the supernatural. It is a river of people who have received the abundance of God and are unashamed of all of God's power.

Have you ventured into the river?

Are you ankle deep?

Have you come in knee deep?

Have you waded up to the waist?

As long as you are ankle deep, knee deep, or only waist deep, you still have your feet on the bottom. You still are trying to determine your own destiny. You can get out of the water whenever you choose. You can stay close to the edge. You are running your own life. You are in the flow of God, but the flow is not in you!

Come on out into the deeper water! Take your feet off the bottom. Let the river of the Spirit take you wherever God wants you to go. It is safe. You can trust the move of the Holy Spirit. You can trust God.

God wants you to have a full measure of His abundance and the power of the Holy Spirit. He wants you to be a supernatural witness to this world. As long as you try to please others only, you cannot believe God. But when you just want to honor and please God alone, you can believe God for all things!

The Lord is asking, "Will you come into the deep waters of this river of spiritual life?"

Make your choice. Trust God completely with your life! Let the Spirit of God baptize you with power. Let the river of God take you into the fullness of His abundance.

God wants you to have

a full measure of His abundance

and the power

of the Holy Spirit.

Reflections from JOEL

The psalmist said, "Oh, taste and see that the Lord is good; blessed is the man who trusts in Him!" (Psalm 34:8).

Too many of us go through life with a weak, powerless mentality. Every time we shrink back and say, "Well, I can't do it; I don't have what it takes," we're conforming to it. When we allow ourselves to be full of fear, worry, or anxiety, or when we are uptight about something, we're surrendering to a weak mentality instead of allowing the Holy Spirit to help and empower us.

It's time to step up to God's dining table and dig in to the fabulous banquet He has prepared for you, complete with every good thing imaginable. God has everything you need—joy, forgiveness, restoration, peace, healing—everything you need to live at your full potential. It's all waiting for you at God's banquet table, if you'll pull up your chair and take the place He has prepared for you.

Best of all, the price has already been paid.

CHAPTER ONE

An Abundance *of* Grace *for* Your Every Need

Sometimes we tend to think that everything depends entirely upon us and what we can do. As a result, we become frustrated and disappointed with our lives. If the apostle Paul had considered his past as a persecutor of the church, he would have been discouraged. But he was able to say, "But by the grace of God I am what I am, and His grace toward me was not in vain; but I labored more abundantly than they all, yet not I, but the grace of God which was with me" (1 Corinthians 15:10).

The word *grace* appears approximately 40 times in the Old Testament and 150 times in the New Testament. Grace is God's undeserved favor upon our lives, and as we see so graphically in the life of Paul, it is the foundation of the Christian life.

When Paul greeted the churches in his epistles, he often began by saying, "Grace to you and peace from God our Father and the Lord Jesus Christ." Usually, he closed his letters by writing, "The grace of our Lord Jesus be with you." Paul knew how much the believers needed the grace of God to live out the Gospel in their daily lives—our spiritual lives start and finish by His grace.

Dominion Lost Through the Fall

God created Adam to reign in life, and He gave him dominion over all the earth. He gave Adam a free will, or the power of choice. Then God put something in the Garden to allow him to exercise the power of choice. The choice was whether to obey or disobey God. When Adam sinned, death reigned on this earth, as was stated so clearly in Romans 5:17.

God has given every man and woman the power of choice. We can choose to believe God's Word, or we can choose to believe a lie of Satan.

Satan came in the form of a beautiful serpent to tempt Eve. Today, he comes to tempt people in many different areas. He may even come as an angel of light (2 Corinthians 11:14).

The moment Adam lost his authority and dominion, the great love of God began to act on behalf of all mankind. God never intended for man to go through life under the authority of Satan or any of his dark powers. God told Satan that He would break his lordship through the seed of the woman, and that He would use man to bruise his head. "Because you have done this, you are cursed more than all cattle, and more than every beast of the field; on your belly you shall go, and you shall eat dust all the days of your life. And I will put enmity between you and the woman, and between your seed and her Seed; He shall bruise your head, and you shall bruise His heel" (Genesis 3:14–15).

Jesus came to earth and defeated Satan on the cross of Calvary, and then He said to us:

> "BEHOLD, I GIVE YOU THE AUTHORITY
> *to trample on serpents and scorpions,*
> *and over all the power of the enemy, and nothing*
> *shall by any means hurt you"* (LUKE 10:19).
> *What Adam lost, Jesus has restored*
> *to us through His grace.*

God Looks at Us Through Eyes of Grace

In Genesis we read that as man began to multiply on the face of the earth, God saw that the wickedness of man was great in the earth, and his thoughts were continually evil (Genesis 6:5). "So the Lord said, 'I will destroy man whom I have created from the face of the earth, both man and beast, creeping thing and birds of the air, for I am sorry that I have made them'" (Genesis 6:7).

God knows what is in a man's heart. He knows our thoughts (Psalm 139:2).

Throughout the Bible, we learn that God looks at His people through eyes of grace. He looks at our hearts (Proverbs 21:2). He knows our motives, and when no one else can see anything attractive about us, He begins to move on our behalf. "For the eyes of the Lord run to and fro throughout the whole earth, to show Himself strong on behalf of those whose heart is loyal to Him" (2 Chronicles 16:9).

Have you ever considered a farm pasture in the winter months? Its grass is usually brown and unattractive—very insignificant. In fact, you could pass that field day after day and not even notice it. But in the springtime, when the rains fall and the sun begins to shine on that field, the grass turns green and it becomes a lush pastureland.

That field is an example of the grace of God. You may feel that you are an insignificant person—someone the world has never noticed. But God sees and loves you. The Son of God begins to shine upon you, and you not only become attractive to God, but to those around you. You begin to reproduce and bear fruit.

Noah's life was a demonstration of the grace of God. "But Noah found grace in the eyes of the LORD. This is the genealogy of Noah. Noah was a just man, perfect in his generations. Noah walked with God" (Genesis 6:8–9). Noah may have been unnoticed by his generation, but he was noticed by God. He may have been considered insignificant to those around him, but he was significant to God. The eyes of the Lord rested upon Noah, and when he began to hear God speak to him, he obeyed His voice. God showered His grace on Noah and spared him and his family from the destructive Flood.

Abraham found favor in the eyes of the Lord. "So he lifted his eyes and looked, and behold, three men were standing by him; and when he saw them, he ran from the tent door to meet them, and bowed himself to the ground, and said, 'My Lord, if I have now found favor in Your sight, do not pass on by Your servant'" (Genesis 18:2–3).

The eyes of the Lord rested on Abraham, and similar to Noah, Abraham began to hear God speak to him. "I will make you exceedingly fruitful; and I will make nations of you, and kings shall come from you. And I will establish My covenant between Me and you and your descendants after you in their generations, for an everlasting covenant, to be God to you and your descendants after you" (Genesis 17:6–7).

We are the seed of Abraham. God's covenant with Abraham is our covenant. When God looked at Abraham, He not only saw Abraham; He also saw you and me. "And if you are Christ's, then you are Abraham's seed, and heirs according to the promise" (Galatians 3:29). God saw us reigning in life as kings, heirs with Christ.

The life of Joseph beautifully exemplifies the grace of God. Despite the fact that his envious brothers sold him into slavery in Egypt and that he was locked away in prison on false charges by Potiphar's wife, "The keeper of the prison did not look into anything that was under Joseph's authority, because the

God knows what is in a man's heart. He knows our thoughts.

LORD was with him; and whatever he did, the LORD made it prosper" (Genesis 39:23). God gave Joseph the grace and favor and wisdom to interpret prophetic dreams for Pharaoh, and Joseph ended up being placed in charge of the royal granaries and was made an official next in rank to Pharaoh himself. God placed Joseph in a position to provide food that saved Egypt as well as his own family from a famine that affected the whole world. That is amazing grace and living in the abundance of God!

GOD HEARS OUR CRIES AND MEETS OUR NEEDS

Joseph, his brothers, and all that generation died in Egypt, but the Israelite families were fruitful and multiplied so greatly that the land was filled with them. Then a new king, who did not know Joseph, came to power in Egypt. He feared their numbers and put slave masters over all the Israelites. However, the more they were oppressed, the more they multiplied and spread. Eventually, the edict came—every newborn Jewish boy was to be thrown into the river, but every newborn girl could live.

God saw us reigning in life as kings, heirs with Christ.

Before his death, Joseph had spoken a promise to his brothers. "I am dying; but God will surely visit you, and bring you out of this land to the land of which He swore to Abraham, to Isaac, and to Jacob" (Genesis 50:24).

When God encourages His people to seek His face, He is urging them to live in such a way that His eyes can be turned in their direction. "The eyes of the Lord are on the righteous, and His ears are open to their cry" (Psalm 34:15). This is what happened to the children of Israel when they were in bondage in Egypt. God heard their cries.

As a baby, Moses' life was not only graciously spared by Pharaoh's daughter, but she adopted him and provided him with the training of the most advanced nation in civilization at the time. Moses was instructed in all the wisdom of the Egyptians.

Years later, Moses visited his own people and observed them in bondage of slavery. He saw an Egyptian beating a Hebrew, one of his own people, and in anger, he killed the Egyptian and hid him in the sand. When Pharaoh heard this, he tried to kill Moses, but Moses fled to Midian. There he lived for forty years learning the ways of the wilderness, its resources, and its climate. God was preparing Moses to spend the next forty years in the wilderness with the Israelites.

It was here that Moses saw the burning bush and God began to speak with him. "And the LORD said: 'I have surely seen the oppression of My people who are in Egypt, and have heard their cry because of their taskmasters, for I know their sorrows. So I have come down to deliver them out of the hand of the Egyptians, and to bring them up from that land to a good and large land, to a land flowing with milk and honey . . .'" (Exodus 3:7–8).

God gave specific instructions through Moses for each household of Israel to sacrifice one spotless lamb and to place the blood of that lamb on the doorpost of their house. The blood of the lamb was a sign for the death angel to pass over that house. This sacrifice is known as the Passover. "Now the blood shall be a sign for you on the houses where you are. And when I see the blood, I will pass over you; and the plague shall not be on you to destroy you when I strike the land of Egypt" (Exodus 12:13).

God, through Moses, brought deliverance to His people through His gracious provision for their greatest needs, starting with their salvation.

We Have Found Grace Upon Grace Through Jesus!

The Lord Jesus Christ came to earth and offered Himself as our sacrificial Lamb. It was at the cross, through the shedding of the blood of the spotless Lamb of God, that the grace of God was offered not to one man, not to one nation, but to all who would receive Him. "But the free gift is not like the offense. For if by the one man's offense many died, much more the grace of God and the gift by the grace of the one Man, Jesus Christ, abounded to many" (Romans 5:15).

The Bible teaches us that all men died spiritually when Adam sinned. God, through Jesus Christ, brings life to all who will receive Him. His grace is out of all proportion to the fall of man. The first Adam was made a living soul; the last Adam (Jesus) was made a life-giving Spirit. "For if by the one man's offense death reigned through the one, much more those who receive abundance of grace and of the gift of righteousness will reign in life through the One, Jesus Christ" (Romans 5:17).

Through the grace of God, we have received the Spirit of Christ. We are no longer dead in our trespasses and sins. We have received an abundance of grace. "For the grace of God that brings salvation has appeared to all men" (Titus 2:11).

The prophet Jeremiah foretold the restoration of God's people. He could see the church of Jesus Christ through the eyes of faith. "For I will set My eyes on them for good, and I will bring them back to this land; I will build them and not pull them down, and I will plant them and not pluck them up. Then I will give them a heart to know Me, that I am the LORD; and they shall be My people, and I will be their God, for they shall return to Me with their whole heart" (Jeremiah 24:6–7).

God has looked upon His church, and we have found grace in His sight! The prophet Isaiah also saw the glory of the church. "'As for Me,' says the LORD, 'this is My covenant with them: My Spirit who is upon you, and My words which I have put in your mouth, shall not depart from your mouth, nor from the mouth of your descendants, nor from the mouth of your descendants' descendants,' says the LORD, 'from this time and forevermore. Arise, shine; for your light has come! And the glory of the LORD is risen upon you. For behold, the darkness shall cover the earth, and deep darkness the people; but the LORD will arise over you, and His glory will be seen upon you'" (Isaiah 59:21—60:2).

Isaiah prophesied that there would come forth a stem of Jesse and the Spirit of the Lord would rest upon Him:

> *the spirit of wisdom,*
> *the spirit of understanding,*
> *the spirit of counsel,*
> *the spirit of might,*
> *the spirit of knowledge,*
> *and the fear of the Lord.*

Isaiah said that Jesus, this stem of Jesse, would not judge after the sight of His eyes, neither reprove after the hearing of His ears (Isaiah 11:1–4). God sent Jesus into the world that we might become like Him. He is our perfect example. He dwelt among us that we might know Him. "But as many as received Him, to them He gave the right to become children of God, to those who believe in His name: who were born, not of blood, nor of the will of the flesh, nor of the will of man, but of God. . . . And of His fullness we have all received, and grace for grace. For the law was given through Moses, but grace and truth came through Jesus Christ" (John 1:12–13, 16–17).

By the grace of God that came through Jesus Christ, we have the power to become the sons of God. We can be led by the Spirit of God. We can have the spirit of wisdom, understanding, counsel, might, knowledge, and the fear of the Lord. We do not have to judge after what our eyes see or our ears hear. Our direction comes from within us—through the Spirit of God who resides in our spirits.

God sent Jesus into the world that we might become like Him.

THE GRACE OF GOD IS FREE!

We cannot earn the grace of God. We cannot work for His favor. We can never make ourselves acceptable to God. We must receive His grace through faith and come to God as we are.

The Bible teaches us that while we were dead in sin, Jesus made us alive. A dead man cannot work! A dead man cannot earn anything! "But God, who is rich in mercy, because of His great love with which He loved us, even when we were dead in trespasses, made us alive together with Christ (by grace you have been saved), and raised

us up together, and made us sit together in the heavenly places in Christ Jesus, that in the ages to come He might show the exceeding riches of His grace in His kindness toward us in Christ Jesus. For by grace you have been saved through faith, and that not of yourselves; it is the gift of God, not of works, lest anyone should boast" (Ephesians 2:4–9).

We are saved by grace through faith; that is by believing that salvation is a free gift.

Grace is a gift of God. We cannot boast about it.

Grace originates with God. It cannot be achieved by works. "Now to him who works, the wages are not counted as grace but as debt. But to him who does not work but believes on Him who justifies the ungodly, his faith is accounted for righteousness" (Romans 4:4–5).

We must stop working and trying to be justified and start believing that we *are* justified! That is when God counts us righteous.

We cannot earn the grace of God.

We cannot work for His favor.

GOD'S GRACE IS ALWAYS SUFFICIENT

When we receive Jesus Christ, we receive the total grace of God. In every situation in which we realize we need grace, Jesus is the source.

We are no match for the enemy in our own strength. Our emotions and our minds and our wills are not the tool with which we defeat the devil. We do not have the power to live the Christian life on our own.

God's grace begins where our ability ends. When the situation is impossible, if you will believe, you will see the grace of God manifested.

If you are tempted to be angry, allow Jesus to demonstrate His peace (Colossians 3:15).

If you are tempted to doubt, remember the life you now live is by faith in Him (Galatians 2:20).

If you are tempted to give up, believe that you have His strength to go on (Philippians 4:13).

God's grace is always sufficient! "Concerning this thing I pleaded with the Lord three times that it might depart from me. And He said to me, 'My grace is sufficient for you, for My strength is made perfect in weakness.' Therefore most gladly I will rather boast in my infirmities, that the power of Christ may rest upon me. Therefore I take pleasure in infirmities, in reproaches, in needs, in persecutions, in distresses, for Christ's sake. For when I am weak, then I am strong" (2 Corinthians 12:8–10).

Should we not say as Paul said, "I take pleasure in the midst of my need, because I know that His grace is sufficient. God will meet my needs, whether they are spiritual, physical, mental, marital, or financial. Not only will He meet my needs, but through this experience I will gain confidence in knowing Him."

"And God is able to make all grace abound toward you, that you, always having all sufficiency in all things, may have an abundance for every good work" (2 Corinthians 9:8).

There is no insufficiency in Jesus. His grace is sufficient in all circumstances.

We reign in life as kings through the abundance of grace!

Reflections from
JOEL

I love how the Amplified Bible renders Ephesians 2:7: "He did this that He might clearly demonstrate through the ages to come the immeasurable (limitless, surpassing) riches of His free grace (His unmerited favor) in [His] kindness and goodness of heart toward us in Christ Jesus."

God wants this to be the best time of your life. But if you are going to receive this favor, you must enlarge your vision. You can't go around thinking negative, defeated, limiting thoughts. "Well, I've gone as far as my career will allow." Or, "I've had this problem for so long; I guess it's just a part of me."

To experience God's immeasurable favor, His grace, you must start expecting His blessings. Start thinking bigger. Get rid of any old negative mindset. If you will make room for increase in your own thinking, God will bring those things to pass. But God will not pour fresh, creative ideas and blessings into old attitudes. Expect God's grace to abound toward you today and in every situation.

CHAPTER TWO

An Abundance *of* Forgiveness *for* Every Relationship

One day I was talking to the Lord about healing. I had been thinking of the healings Jesus performed while He was on earth. I said, "Lord, You were such a great healing preacher. I wish I could have been there to hear some of Your healing sermons."

The Lord said to me, "You have them in the Bible. Read Matthew, Mark, Luke, and John. That is what I taught. If the people believed and acted on My words, they were healed. If they listened to Me and refused to believe what I taught, I could not heal them, even though I was there in person."

I realized that in the Gospels, I had the healing sermons of Jesus. I am sure those are not all of His sermons, but they are the ones that God knew we needed.

When I teach what Jesus taught in the Bible, people receive lasting healings and miracles from God. The truths that Jesus taught in the Bible usually do not make people run and jump with joy. They are serious subjects that have to be dealt with in every area of life.

The Power of Forgiveness

Jesus had much to say about forgiveness. "Moreover if your brother sins against you, go and tell him his fault between you and him alone. If he hears you, you have gained your brother. But if he will not hear, take with you one or two more, that 'by the mouth of two or three witnesses every word may be established'" (Matthew 18:15–16).

It is not strange that Jesus would preach about brothers having fights and disagreements. Jesus' teachings got down to the real nitty-gritty of life.

Peter heard Jesus say that, and he could not get the concept of forgiveness out of his mind. You can tell it was bugging him. "Then Peter came to Him and said, 'Lord, how often shall my brother sin against me, and I forgive him? Up to seven times?' Jesus said to him, 'I do not say to you, up to seven times, but up to seventy times seven'" (Matthew 18:21–22).

Jesus said we are to forgive our brother or sister four hundred and ninety times! In other words, forgiveness is an attitude; it is a way of life.

I remember a fellow who treated me so badly that I felt like giving him a piece of my mind! After he had wronged me, I wrote him a real nasty letter, letting him have it with both barrels, but once I was finished, I tore it up. I had to forgive him. Jesus gave me no other choice.

When we learn to forgive others as God has forgiven us, we will reign in life as kings over every heartache, hurt, and situation, and we can enjoy the abundance God has provided for us.

THE UNHAPPY TRUTH ABOUT UNFORGIVENESS

After setting Peter straight on the nature of forgiveness, Jesus continued His sermon, explaining the importance of forgiveness in Matthew 18:23–35:

> *"Therefore the kingdom of heaven is like a certain king who wanted to settle accounts with his servants. And when he had begun to settle accounts, one was brought to him who owed him ten thousand talents. But as he was not able to pay, his master commanded that he be sold, with his wife and children and all that he had, and that payment be made. The servant therefore fell down before him,*

saying, 'Master, have patience with me, and I will pay you all.' Then the master of that servant was moved with compassion, released him, and forgave him the debt.

"But that servant went out and found one of his fellow servants who owed him a hundred denarii; and he laid hands on him and took him by the throat, saying, 'Pay me what you owe!' So his fellow servant fell down at his feet and begged him, saying, 'Have patience with me, and I will pay you all.' And he would not, but went and threw him into prison till he should pay the debt. So when his fellow servants saw what had been done, they were very grieved, and came and told their master all that had been done. Then his master, after he had called him, said to him, 'You wicked servant! I forgave you all that debt because you begged me. Should you not also have had compassion on your fellow servant, just as I had pity on you?' And his master was angry, and delivered him to the torturers until he should pay all that was due to him.

"So My heavenly Father also will do to you if each of you, from his heart, does not forgive his brother his trespasses."

This is not my sermon on the power of forgiveness; it is Jesus' sermon. This is not my doctrine; it is the doctrine of Jesus.

There are three important facts about unforgiveness to be learned from this passage of Scripture.

First, the master said that his servant was wicked because he did not forgive his fellow servant. God looks at our failure to forgive others as wickedness. God forgave us from all the sins of our past, and He continues to forgive us when we fall even after we have put our faith in Jesus and been born again by the Holy Spirit. How much should we forgive others!

Second, the master was angry with the servant who did not forgive his fellow servant. Unforgiveness in our lives provokes the anger of God. If we are going to live a life that is pleasing to God, we must live a life of forgiveness.

Third, the master delivered his servant to the tormentors because he had failed to forgive. If we do not forgive, our heavenly Father will have to deal with us in the same way we deal with others.

The place of torment is not hell. Thank God, Jesus paid the debt for us, and we do not have to go to hell. But if we continue to live in unforgiveness toward someone, the Bible says that God will deliver us over to the tormentors until we pay our debt. And Jesus, talking about His wonderful, righteous, loving, and merciful Father, said, "So My heavenly Father also will do to you if each of you, from his heart, does not forgive his brother his trespasses."

That is not shouting for joy ground; it is sober ground. That is the Head of the church speaking directly to our hearts. Jesus is teaching us how to avoid being delivered to the tormentors.

Jesus said that a child of God can be delivered over to the tormentors until he pays for his wrongdoings. He can be delivered to the tormentors until he forgives!

There is physical, mental, and spiritual torment. Physical torment is sickness and disease in our bodies. Mental torment produces fear and confusion. Spiritual torment is being accused by Satan. He is the accuser of the brethren (Revelation 12:10).

Forgiveness and Healing Are Closely Related

I knew a pastor whose fingers were bent over and twisted with arthritis. He said, "Pastor Osteen, one day I made a decision to start living a life of forgiveness." Every time he thought of someone toward whom he had a wrong attitude, he would forgive that person. He said, "I would lie in bed and think of people as I prayed. If someone came to my mind, I would forgive them. As I drove the car, if someone came to my mind, I would forgive them."

Several months after he made his decision to live in forgiveness, finger after finger straightened up, and healing came into his body. Eventually, he was completely healed! God did not send the sickness, but this pastor's obedience unlocked the door to healing in his life. God is pleased with us when we forgive.

Jesus said, "Therefore I say to you, whatever things you ask when you pray, believe that you receive them, and you will have them. And whenever you stand praying, if you have anything against anyone, forgive him, that your Father in heaven may also forgive you your trespasses. But if you do not forgive, neither will your Father in heaven forgive your trespasses" (Mark 11:24–26).

There was a woman in our church who had a large tumor. Based upon James 5:14–15, we anointed her with oil, laid hands on her, and prayed for her, but she did not get healed. Later on, in one of our church services, I taught on this principle of forgiveness. Afterward this woman came to me and said, "I did not know that unforgiveness was locked away in my heart. I had no idea that I had anything against anyone."

Many times people who are seeking healing need to walk in forgiveness.

She continued, "The Holy Spirit brought my mother-in-law to my mind and something that happened years ago. I was not aware that I held anything against her, but the Holy Spirit showed me that I had resentment locked away in the recesses of my heart. I had never truly forgiven her."

After she forgave her mother-in-law for whatever had happened years before, the tumor disappeared.

When you open yourself up to God and say, "God, search my heart and show me how I can change," He will help you.

Forgiveness and *healing* are closely related. Many times people who are seeking healing really need to walk in forgiveness.

Forgive and be healed! It may not always happen instantly, but it will happen!

The Responsibility to Forgive Is Ours

Many divorced people have a battle with unforgiveness. It is easy for a wife to have bitterness against a husband who has mistreated her. It is easy for a husband to have resentment against a wife who has left him. I have heard more than one wife say, "He is guilty. He ruined my life! He left me without anything. I had to take care of the children myself."

That wife is right; he is guilty. But only the guilty need mercy. Guilty people must be forgiven, not for their sakes, but for ours! Why? Jesus tells us: "For if you forgive men their trespasses, your heavenly Father will also forgive you. But if you do not forgive men their trespasses, neither will your Father forgive your trespasses" (Matthew 6:14–15).

If you forgive, *you will be forgiven.*

If you do not forgive, *you will not be forgiven.*

There is no alternative. God will only forgive us as we forgive others.

Jesus put the responsibility upon us to initiate the forgiveness. In the Lord's Prayer, Jesus again mentioned forgiveness: "And forgive us our debts, as we forgive our debtors" (Matthew 6:12).

Resentment, bitterness, and unforgiveness release a negative force within our entire beings. It is a very dangerous force that grows stronger each day we choose not to follow the teachings of Jesus.

The relationship between you and other members of your family is very important. The relationship between a mother-in-law and daughter-in-law is an area where there needs to be a searching of the heart; likewise, between mother-in-law and son-in-law, between parents and children, and between brothers and sisters.

One day, as I allowed the Holy Spirit to search my heart for anything that He might find offensive, He showed me that I had held things against my mother and daddy. They quarreled a lot when I was a child, and I grew up resenting the tension that it produced in my heart and in our home. I lived in fear of them divorcing. I remember many times crying over their disputes.

As the Lord began to speak to me about the critical thoughts I had toward my parents, He reminded me that when I was a boy, my parents did not have an automatic washing machine. They did not have many of the conveniences that are plentiful in our day. We had a large family, and it had not been easy for my parents to raise us during the Great Depression. My heart was broken because of my wrong attitude.

I was a successful minister. God had blessed my life in many ways, yet I still had areas of unforgiveness in my heart. Opening my heart to the Lord Jesus, I saw those unpleasant memories were actually areas of un-forgiveness.

Parents have to be willing to forgive their children. Perhaps your children have really hurt you badly. They may be guilty of some terrible wrongs, but you must forgive. As you forgive them, you will be forgiven, and healing will come to your spirit, mind, and body.

"IF YOU HAVE ANYTHING AGAINST ANYONE"

When you walk in forgiveness, you open the door for God to work in your life and in the lives of those who have wronged you. As you forgive, you will reign in life as a king over circumstances, disappointments, and sorrow. Forgiveness is a key to enjoying the abundance of God.

Forgiveness produces:

> Peace,
> reconciliation,
> harmony,
> understanding,
> and fellowship.

Unforgiveness produces:

> Strife,
> bitterness,
> disharmony,
> hatred,
> and warfare.

At times, the whole human race is in danger of being overwhelmed by these evil, negative forces. We, as Christians, are to shine as lights in a dark world. We are to be forgiving people. "And whenever you stand praying, if you have anything against anyone, forgive him, that your Father in heaven may also forgive you your trespasses" (Mark 11:25).

Anything means everything, big and small, even what may seem like almost nothing at all.

Anyone means everybody. We are to forgive everybody for anything and everything they have done to hurt us.

Obviously, the most hurtful areas of our lives need to be forgiven. Jesus said the minutest detail must also be forgiven.

Sometimes we need to forgive a person who is dead. Unforgiveness is equally as harmful in our lives whether the person is living or dead.

Many times the hardest person to forgive is oneself. We make many mistakes, some of which may have devastated our lives, yet we have to learn to accept those mistakes as being a part of our past. We have to press on. Jesus taught us to forgive if we have anything against anyone, and that includes ourselves.

GET AT THE ROOT OF THE PROBLEM

People want to receive from God, but they do not want to talk about unforgiveness. They may want to be healed or to be blessed with a new job or to have all of their financial needs met. Unforgiveness is often the root of the problem.

When Jesus was in Bethany, He passed a fig tree. "And seeing from afar a fig tree having leaves, He went to see if perhaps He would find something on it. When He came to it, He found nothing but leaves, for it was not the season for figs. In response Jesus said to it, 'Let no one eat fruit from you ever again.' And His disciples heard it" (Mark 11:13–14).

There were two areas of that fig tree—the *seen* and the *unseen*. There was a part that they could see and a part they could not see. The part that could not be seen was the root system.

We have a root system. Our root system is the unseen part of us—the spirit person.

When Jesus spoke to that fig tree, His words took effect in the unseen area. By the following day, the fig tree had withered, and His words had manifested in the seen area. Jesus knew that the unseen area was where the tree received its life. The Word of the Lord took effect immediately in the unseen area, the root system.

If we want results in the seen area—our physical bodies—we must learn to care for the root system properly.

The Bible teaches us that bitterness has a root: "Pursue peace with all people, and holiness, without which no one will see the Lord: looking carefully lest anyone fall short of the grace of God; lest any root of bitterness springing up cause trouble, and by this many become defiled" (Hebrews 12:14–15).

You Have the Power to Forgive

You may say, "I do not have the power to forgive. I was so mistreated as a child that I could never forgive my parents for what they did." Yes, you can. You can forgive because God provided forgiveness at the cross for you. You are forgiven, not because you deserve it, but by grace.

By the grace provided at the cross, you have the power necessary to forgive others. Isaiah 53:4–6 makes that perfectly clear:

Surely He has borne our griefs
And carried our sorrows;
Yet we esteemed Him stricken,
Smitten by God, and afflicted.
But He was wounded for our transgressions,
He was bruised for our iniquities;
The chastisement for our peace
*   was upon Him,*
And by His stripes we are healed.
All we like sheep have gone astray;
We have turned, every one, to his own way;
And the LORD has laid on Him
*   the iniquity of us all.*

Only on the basis of the atoning death of Jesus Christ on the cross can we receive forgiveness from God.

Only on the basis of the grace of God offered to us by His death can we offer forgiveness to others.

It was at the cross that Jesus cancelled every claim of sin on our lives, and it is at the cross that we are empowered by grace to forgive. "But God forbid that I should boast except in the cross of our Lord Jesus Christ, by whom the world has been crucified to me, and I to the world" (Galatians 6:14).

Forgiveness is a *decision*. You must choose to forgive whether you feel like it or not. As you stand on that decision, God in you will love the person who has wronged you. One day, you may suddenly realize that you cannot even remember the wrong they committed against you.

Receiving the forgiveness of God is also a *decision*. You choose to believe that God's Word is true. If God said He would forgive you, He will. You do not deserve it, but forgiveness is yours because He loves you and desires fellowship with you. There is no condemnation to those who are in Christ Jesus (Romans 8:1).

Forgiveness

IS A DECISION.

A PRAYER FOR FORGIVENESS

David prayed a beautiful prayer for the forgiveness of his sins. In Psalm 51:1–3, 6–13, he desired to be set apart to God:

> *Have mercy upon me, O God,*
> *According to Your lovingkindness;*
> *According to the multitude of Your tender mercies,*
> *Blot out my transgressions.*
> *Wash me thoroughly from my iniquity,*
> *And cleanse me from my sin.*
> *For I acknowledge my transgressions,*
> *And my sin is always before me.*
> *Behold, You desire truth in the inward parts,*
> *And in the hidden part You will make me*
> * to know wisdom.*
> *Purge me with hyssop, and I shall be clean;*
> *Wash me, and I shall be whiter than snow.*
> *Make me hear joy and gladness,*
> *That the bones You have broken may rejoice.*
> *Hide Your face from my sins,*
> *And blot out all my iniquities.*

Create in me a clean heart, O God,
And renew a steadfast spirit within me.
Do not cast me away from Your presence,
And do not take Your Holy Spirit from me.
Restore to me the joy of Your salvation,
And uphold me by Your generous Spirit.
Then I will teach transgressors Your ways,
And sinners shall be converted to You.

We can pray the same prayer that David prayed. The Bible says that David was a man after God's own heart.

Praise God, we have been forgiven, and we have the power to forgive others through Jesus Christ!

We reign in life through forgiveness! We walk in the abundance of His provisions!

Reflections from JOEL

A young woman once came to my dad for spiritual help. Several boys had sexually assaulted her when she was in her teens. Consequently, she could not have an intimate relationship with her husband. She realized that all that anger and hatred in her heart was affecting her relationship with her husband. She knew it wasn't going to be easy to forgive those men, but she refused to let the past continue to poison her present or future. Interestingly, from that moment of forgiveness on, she was able to enjoy a healthy relationship with her husband. She got down to the root to deal with the fruit.

To live in the present moment, we must forgive those people who have hurt us in the past. Too often, we try to collect our debts from other people. When somebody hurts us, we feel like they owe us. Somebody should pay for that pain we have suffered! So we take it out on other people even though they weren't involved.

But here's the problem: only God can pay that debt; other people can't do it. Moreover, you should not drag something that happened in the past into your relationships today. Don't punish your spouse, your children, your friends, or your coworkers for something in your past. Instead, turn it over to God and keep your heart free from bitterness and resentment.

CHAPTER THREE

An Abundance
of Righteousness
for Every
Accusation
of Satan

Until a man is righteous, and *knows* that he is righteous, he will not live in the abundance of God and reign in life. "For if by the one man's offense death reigned through the one, much more those who receive abundance of grace and of the gift of righteousness will reign in life through the One, Jesus Christ" (Romans 5:17).

We must be informed from God's Word of what belongs to us and learn to honor God by the way we live. God is not pleased when we disregard any of the great redemptive work of Jesus. He desires to bring us out of the realm of slavery and servitude and into our rightful position in the kingdom of God.

We must know:

> *We are redeemed.*
> *We are new creation beings.*
> *We are delivered from Satan's power.*
> *We are free of all our sins.*

The moment we receive Jesus as our personal Savior, we receive God's nature and become the righteousness of God in Christ Jesus. "For He made Him who knew no sin to be sin for us, that we might become the righteousness of God in Him" (2 Corinthians 5:21).

Jesus became sin for us. As a result, we can stand in the presence of Almighty God free of sin—righteous and holy children of God. He no longer looks at us as sinners. He sees us as the righteousness of God in Christ Jesus.

However, a sense of unworthiness, no matter how it is produced in our lives, destroys faith, robs us of our peace of mind, and makes us ineffectual Christians. It is a work of the enemy to keep us from living in the abundance of God as kings and priests.

If we have a feeling of inferiority, we cannot reign in life. We are *in Christ*. That is our position by faith. We have been bought with a price, with the precious blood of Jesus, and we no longer belong to ourselves (1 Corinthians 6:19–20).

All of our success is in Him. We cannot fail when we understand that we have been made righteous.

Joined to Jesus Christ, we have no room for thoughts and feelings of inferiority.

Joined to Jesus Christ, the exalted Son of God, we have no room for thoughts and feelings of inferiority. We must replace those feelings with the knowledge of who we are in Christ Jesus.

Countless believers live under a constant sense of condemnation, feeling they will never be good enough to go to heaven or do anything for His glory. Many sincere and dedicated believers, for instance, have been

taught to believe certain doctrines and ideas that keep them in bondage and torment. I once talked with a woman who had been told that she would go to hell if she put on lipstick or cut her hair, and she was experiencing severe emotional problems over it. That may seem extreme, but many believers carry religious baggage that keeps them from living in Christ's righteousness.

Let us examine two aspects of righteousness: the Divine Side and the Practical Application.

THE DIVINE SIDE

God, through Jesus Christ, has redeemed us from sin and shame: ". . . even the righteousness of God, through faith in Jesus Christ, to all and on all who believe. For there is no difference; for all have sinned and fall short of the glory of God, being justified freely by His grace through the redemption that is in Christ Jesus" (Romans 3:22–24).

Our righteousness comes only through faith in Christ Jesus. We have all sinned, but when we stand at the foot of the cross, we stand on level ground. We observe the cross and embrace it with the knowledge that we have sinned, and because of our faith in what He has done, we are forgiven and cleansed from all sin and unrighteousness.

Righteousness, being made just and holy before God, comes to us as a free gift. We can never earn it. We will never be good enough to receive it. It does not come by external observances—by keeping the list of dos and don'ts or wearing the proper clothing or not wearing lipstick—it only comes to us by faith in Christ Jesus.

In the beginning, man was created to be a king who was subject only to his Creator, but:

> *Man transgressed.*
> *He was disloyal to God.*
> *Man believed Satan.*
> *He believed the devil's lie instead of the Word of God.*
> *Man lost dominion over his own kingdom.*
> *Satan became the ruler of this world and the prince of the power of the air.*
> *Satan took over the entire kingdom that God had commissioned to Adam.*
> *Instead of living in the abundance of God as a king, man became a slave.*
> *He became a slave to sin and Satan.*

The Practical Application

Every person must choose to live like a king, or he or she will automatically exist as a slave.

We have the power of choice to change our destiny! We should choose a personal relationship with Jesus. If we choose to live by rules and outward appearances, we are not going to live as kings in the abundance of God.

In his letter to the Romans, Paul tells us that the Gospel is for the salvation of all men (1:16). God has given to every man the same measure of faith to believe on the Lord Jesus Christ (12:3).

"But the righteousness of faith speaks in this way, 'Do not say in your heart, "Who will ascend into heaven?"' (that is, to bring Christ down from above) or, '"Who will descend into the abyss?"' (that is, to bring Christ up from the dead). But what does it say? 'The word is near you, in your mouth and in your heart' (that is, the word of faith which we preach): that if you confess with your mouth the Lord Jesus and believe in your heart that God has raised Him from the dead, you will be saved. For *with the heart one believes unto righteousness, and with the mouth confession is made unto salvation*" (Romans 10:6–10).

This is the practical application of righteousness. The righteousness that is of faith speaks! I want you to say out loud: "I Am Righteous!" Say it again, and say it again. Confess it as the truth and believe it in your heart!

We are able to come before the Father and worship Him because of what Jesus has done for us. We do not come in our own righteousness or our own goodness. We could never be good enough even to please ourselves. We come because we are the righteousness of God in Christ Jesus by faith.

THE DIVINE SIDE

God through Jesus Christ has made us new creation beings. "Therefore, if anyone is in Christ, he is a new creation; old things have passed away; behold, all things have become new" (2 Corinthians 5:17).

God said, "Let Us make man in Our image, according to Our likeness . . ." (Genesis 1:26). Man was created to show forth the likeness of God.

When Jesus came to earth as a man, He demonstrated to us the outward appearance of God. He also demonstrated to us the inward spiritual and moral nature of God. Jesus was God in a human body.

When Adam disobeyed God, the inner man died, but the outer man continued to live.

There are two families that dwell on the earth today—the family of God and the family of the devil. We are either the children of God or the children of the devil. "You are of your father the devil, and the desires of your father you want to do. He was a murderer from the beginning, and does not stand in the truth, because there is no truth in him. When he speaks a lie, he speaks from his own resources, for he is a liar and the father of it" (John 8:44).

The Practical Application

Every man must choose to let the inner man dominate his life.

If we are going to live like kings and enjoy the abundance of God, our spirits must be in control. Given a choice to love or to hate, our spirits will choose love. Given a choice to be encouraged or to be discouraged, we will choose to be encouraged. These decisions come out of the newly created spirit—the inner man through the Holy Spirit. You can strengthen the inner man as you study the Word of God and begin to see what God says about you.

There is a story about a great roaring lion and a little puppy. No one would ask, "Which one do you think can whip the other one?" What a foolish question.

However, you could change the outcome of that fight. All you would need to do is stop feeding the lion and start feeding the puppy. If you were patient and continually fed that puppy week after week, he would become strong and healthy. After a time, the lion would become so weak that he could no longer lift his paw.

When you become a Christian, your inner nature is like that little puppy. It must be fed, taught, and trained. Your outer, fleshly nature, like the lion, must be starved until it has no strength.

The people who do not live in the abundance of God are those who feed the lion. They spend very little time in Bible study and prayer. They are unconcerned about attending a good Bible teaching church. Some sit in front of the television and computer screen and feed their carnal natures by the hour. The old lion roars, and they wonder why they do not walk in victory.

What you feed your spirit is important. The new inner spirit will not grow as you eat a steak. It must have spiritual food, and there is only one source. "It is the Spirit who gives life; the flesh profits nothing. The words that I speak to you are spirit, and they are life" (John 6:63).

The devil's trick is to keep many believers in doctrinal chains and hide the great truths of God from us. For years I was kept in ignorance. As a minister, I walked in all the light I knew for many years. I am sure other denominational ministers are doing all they know to do also, but many of us were kept in ignorance. We trusted our teachers and were not taught the complete truths of God's Word.

We were taught fear and condemnation. We were beaten down and constantly reminded of how weak and unworthy we were. I was taught that part of my responsibility as a preacher was to keeping telling other people just how bad they were. The more I did it, the more acclaim I received. They thought that was good preaching.

It reminds me of the story of a little bird that was hatched in a cage. He did not know anything about life outside of that cage, for he had never been outside. As he grew, he began to notice those appendages on his sides and wondered what they were. One day he learned that his wings would lift up and down. He flapped his wings so fast that he flew into the side of the cage. He did that over and over. Deep inside he heard a little voice saying, "You are not made for a cage." But that was the only life he knew.

Then someone mistakenly left the cage door open, and the bird flew out for the first time. Can't you hear that little bird saying, "This is it! I was made for something bigger than a cage!"

The devil has made certain that the body of Christ is all caged up. We have been fed biblical birdseed when we need meat to become eagles. Millions of Christians are behind cages, locked up in doctrines that say miracles have passed away and the days of supernatural direction are over.

By the power of the Holy Spirit, these cages are being opened, and we are beginning to fly together. We are learning the great truths of the Word of God. We are experiencing the abundant, victorious life of Jesus Christ!

THE DIVINE SIDE

God, through Jesus Christ, has delivered us from Satan's power. "Giving thanks to the Father who has qualified us to be partakers of the inheritance of the saints in the light. He has delivered us from the power of darkness and conveyed us into the kingdom of the Son of His love" (Colossians 1:12–13).

God has delivered us from the authority of Satan. That is not something we need to ask God to do for us. He has already done it! It is an eternal truth. "Beware lest anyone cheat you through philosophy and empty deceit, according to the tradition of men, according to the basic principles of the world, and not according to Christ. . . . and you are complete in Him, who is the head of all principality and power. . . . Having disarmed principalities and powers, He made a public spectacle of them, triumphing over them in it" (Colossians 2:8, 10, 15).

Many times we try to win the battles of life with philosophy or the traditions of men. Jesus has spoiled the principalities and powers, and if we will believe Satan has no power over us, we will reign through Jesus instead of giving into defeat.

THE PRACTICAL APPLICATION

Every Christian must study the Word of God and learn to resist his enemy for himself. The way to do this is through prayer and faith. We must say what the Word of God says. First Peter 5:7–8 says, " . . . casting all your care upon Him, for He cares for you. Be sober, be vigilant; because your adversary the devil walks about like a roaring lion, seeking whom he may devour."

Resist the Devil!

*"Put on the whole armor of God, that you may
be able to stand against the wiles of the devil"
(Ephesians 6:11).*

Know Your Enemy!

*"For we do not wrestle against flesh and blood, but
against principalities, against powers, against the rulers
of the darkness of this age, against spiritual hosts of
wickedness in the heavenly places" (Ephesians 6:12).*

Resist Temptation!

*"Therefore take up the whole armor of God, that you
may be able to withstand in the evil day, and having
done all, to stand" (Ephesians 6:13).*

Know Who You Are in Christ!

*"Stand therefore, having girded your waist with
truth, having put on the breastplate of righteousness"
(Ephesians 6:14).*

CASTING ALL

YOUR CARE UPON HIM,

FOR HE CARES FOR YOU.

BE SOBER, BE VIGILANT.

Be Peaceful!

"And having shod your feet with the preparation of the gospel of peace" (Ephesians 6:15).

Do Not Give Up!

"Above all, taking the shield of faith with which you will be able to quench all the fiery darts of the wicked one" (Ephesians 6:16).

Speak the Word!

"And take the helmet of salvation, and the sword of the Spirit, which is the word of God" (Ephesians 6:17).

Pray Always!

"Praying always with all prayer and supplication in the Spirit, being watchful to this end with all perseverance and supplication for all the saints" (Ephesians 6:18).

GOD WANTS US TO RULE AND REIGN

over Satan in this life through

PRAYER AND FAITH.

The Divine Side

God, through Jesus Christ, has forgiven all our sins. "In Him we have redemption through His blood, the forgiveness of sins, according to the riches of His grace" (Ephesians 1:7).

Our sins are forgiven, not on the basis of the sins we have committed, but on the basis of the riches of His grace. God's grace is rich and free!

Have you ever held a tiny baby? You admire that baby and talk about how sweet it is. That baby has no past. As a newborn Christian, you have no spiritual past.

I don't care what your past was. I do not care how many sins you have committed. When you come to God, your past sins cease to exist.

The Practical Application

Every believer of the Lord Jesus Christ must learn to act on the Word of God instead of on what he sees, feels, or hears.

When it seems that you have failed, do not condemn yourself. "There is therefore now no condemnation to those who are in Christ Jesus, who do not walk according to the flesh, but according to the Spirit" (Romans 8:1).

If you feel that you have missed God or failed your fellowman, do not continue in that state of mind. "But if we walk in the light as He is in the light, we have fellowship with one another, and the blood of Jesus Christ His Son cleanses us from all sin. . . . If we confess our sins, He is faithful and just to forgive us our sins and to cleanse us from all unrighteousness" (1 John 1:7, 9).

Be quick to get back into the light with Christ. Confess your sin and believe that He has cleansed you. "Let the redeemed of the LORD say so, whom He has redeemed from the hand of the enemy" (Psalm 107:2).

The secret to victory is acting fearlessly and confessing boldly! Satan is afraid of you!

> *God, through Jesus Christ, has redeemed you.*
> *God, through Jesus Christ, has made you a new*
> *creature.*
> *God, through Jesus Christ, has delivered you from*
> *Satan's power.*
> *God, through Jesus Christ, has forgiven all your sins.*

That is part of the abundance of God that you can receive and enjoy! We reign in life as kings through the gift of righteousness!

The secret to victory is

ACTING FEARLESSLY

and confessing boldly.

Reflections from
JOEL

In the Living Bible, Ephesians 6:14 says, "You will need . . . the breastplate of God's approval." Every morning, no matter how you feel or what you may have done wrong the day before, you can get up and say, "Father, I thank You that I'm forgiven. I thank You that You approve me and that I am your friend."

If you'll do that, you'll be amazed at what begins to happen. Your whole self-image will change. That heavy load of guilt and condemnation will be lifted off you. You'll get your joy back. You'll go out to meet the day with a whole new attitude. But it does not happen automatically; it is something we must do. Just as we put on our clothes every morning, we need to get up and consciously put on God's approval.

Don't allow a sense of guilt and shame to follow you around. Shake off that sense of unworthiness. You may be dealing with a lot of faults. But remember, God is still working on you. You may not be all you want to be, but at least you can thank God you're not what you used to be. Stop looking at how far you have to go, and take a look at how far you've already come.

CHAPTER FOUR

An Abundance
of Joy
for Your
Heartache
and Pain

Wherever I go, I find that believers misunderstand God's secret formula for all of us to live in the abundance of God and to be victorious in life: simply put, it is joy. When the Bible states, "Do not sorrow, for the joy of the LORD is your strength" (Nehemiah 8:10), they tend to read in the word *happiness* for the word *joy*, which creates a host of problems.

We need to know the difference between happiness and joy. If you were to win a million dollars, you would be extremely happy. But that does not necessarily mean you would experience an ounce of real joy. Our happiness goes up or down according to what happens in our lives—that's an outward thing. But joy is the fruit of our relationship with the Holy Spirit (Galatians 5:22). If we have put our faith in Jesus, the newborn spirit that we have received from God has real joy.

The joy of the Lord, not some happiness that we get from material things or other people, is our strength. And the Bible says, "A merry heart does good, like medicine" (Proverbs 17:22). It is good to have joy and have a merry heart on the inside of you. It doesn't say a merry mind does good; it says a merry heart does good like a medicine.

The psalmist says, "Weeping may endure for a night, but joy comes in the morning" (Psalm 30:5). We all have times of heartache and pain. We all have shed our tears. We all have had our times of sorrow and unhappiness. But if we have the Lord Jesus in our hearts, we may weep for a night, but joy comes. Joy is on its way. Weeping may endure for a night, but joy comes in the morning.

It's wonderful what Habakkuk says: "Though the fig tree may not blossom, nor fruit be on the vines; though the labor of the olive may fail, and the fields yield no food; though the flock may be cut off from the fold, and there be no herd in the stalls—yet I will rejoice in the LORD, I will joy in the God of my salvation" (Habakkuk 3:17–18). In today's words, if your lights go out, your gas is turned off, you can't pay your bills, the doctor says you've got cancer, you've got all kinds of trouble with your in-laws and your out-laws, and every other kind of trouble in the world, it doesn't make any difference. Just make up your mind you're going to rejoice in the Lord!

OUR JOY IS IN THE LORD

We will rejoice in the Lord, not in our heartaches and troubles and life circumstances. If you are joined to the Lord by faith, you can rejoice in the Lord and joy in the God of your salvation. *Salvation* means "deliverance." You can be joyful in the God of your salvation.

I see in Daniel 3 the three young Jewish men—Shadrach, Meshach, and Abed-nego—refusing to bow to King Nebuchadnezzar's golden image and headed for that fiery furnace all bound up. I can hear them shouting, "Hallelujah! Hallelujah! Hallelujah!" If you asked them what they are praising God about, they would say, "We're not praising because we're going into the furnace; we're praising Him because we're coming out!"

I see Daniel refusing to stop praying and being thrown into that lions' den in Daniel 6. Similar to his three friends, Daniel goes down in the den praising God. He has the inner joy of the Lord. If you asked him how he could be so joyful going into the lions' den, he would say, "I'm not rejoicing because I'm going in, but because I'm coming out. I take joy in the God of my salvation."

I see Paul and Silas in Acts 16. They've been beaten with rods and have been put in stocks in the Philippian jail. It looks so bad. It has to feel bad. Yet at midnight they are singing praises to God and praying. If you asked them why they are praising God, they would say, "We're not praising God because we're in jail; we're praising God because we're going to get out of jail."

You see, the joy of the Lord is God's secret formula. We have a secret weapon that can hold us in the storm. We have a supernatural joy that is independent of our circumstances but dependent upon the Word of God.

The joy of the Lord
is God's special formula.

A Constant Reason to Rejoice

This amazing truth of joy is seen vividly in Jesus' words to His disciples: "Then the seventy returned with joy, saying, 'Lord, even the demons are subject to us in Your name.' And He said to them, 'I saw Satan fall like lightning from heaven. Behold, I give you the authority to trample on serpents and scorpions, and over all the power of the enemy, and nothing shall by any means hurt you. Nevertheless do not rejoice in this, that the spirits are subject to you, but rather rejoice because your names are written in heaven'" (Luke 10:17–20).

Be filled with joy that
YOUR NAME
is written in the Lamb's Book of Life!

As wonderful as it is that we are given power over the enemy, Jesus said that we should not get excited about that. That's not the real reason for joy. He said, "Don't rejoice because these defeated demons are subject to you in My Name. It's fine to be glad about that, but that's not the reason to rejoice. Rather, rejoice that your names are written in heaven."

There are many reasons for rejoicing. There are reasons for joy. And one of the greatest reasons in the world that Christians should be filled with joy is that our names are written and enrolled in heaven. Notice that it doesn't say to rejoice that your name is written on some church's membership list. It doesn't say to rejoice that your name is written on some organization. It didn't say rejoice that your name is written in a social register. He said, "If you've got your name written down in the Lamb's Book of Life, there's a reason to rejoice!"

We can have all kinds of trouble and trials and pains in the world and still have joy, because we know that our names are written in heaven and we're headed for an eternity where there's no sighing, no crying, no dying and no death, and no separation. That's a reason for real joy. Come on, rejoice!

In Revelation 13, it states that all the people who worship the Antichrist and take the mark of the Beast are those "whose names have not been written in the Book of Life of the Lamb slain from the foundation of the world" (v. 8). Jesus is "the Lamb of God who takes away the sin of the world" (John 1:29). He is that sacrificial Passover Lamb, the One who fulfilled all the millions of lambs that died with the Jewish ceremonial system pointing forward to the cross. They had many lambs, but John said, "This is *the* Lamb of God. Their lambs just covered their sins. But the Lamb of God takes away the sin of the world."

It's wonderful to know that your sins can be eradicated, taken away forever and forever. Who is enrolled in the Lamb's Book of Life? Not those who are spiritually dead, but those who are spiritually alive. There is a book recorded with all of those who have received eternal life through Jesus Christ. Your religion is not going to help you in death. Your organization is not going to help you in death. Your social standing is not going to help you in death. The question is: is your name written down as one who has bowed the knee to Jesus, surrendered your life to Jesus, and made Him the Lord of your life? And are you in the Lamb's Book of Life? That's what counts.

Rejoice not that you have the gift of prophecy or you cast out demons; rejoice because your name is written in heaven. Come on, rejoice! Yes, you can know your name is written in heaven. If you've made Him the Lord of your life, if you've turned from your sin and committed yourself to living for Jesus all of your days, that's what gives you eternal life and that's what gets your name in that Book of Life in heaven.

Now consider Revelation 20, which brings us to the end when God will bring everyone up before Him. "I saw a great white throne and Him who sat on it, from whose face the earth and the heaven fled away. And there was found no place for them" (v. 11). Every man, woman, and child will stand before that great white throne, and there will be no place to hide. You can hide now in your church, in your organization. You can hide in immorality. You can hide in drugs and alcohol. But when you stand before God, there's no place to hide.

Notice what else it says: "And I saw the dead, small and great" (v. 12). The insignificant ones who had little or nothing are standing right beside the great ones who have been kings and rulers and mighty CEOs and have handled millions and billions of dollars. It will be a leveling place. You might have been great on this earth, but you're just like all the others at that great white throne. With every tick of the clock, you're headed for that meeting.

"And I saw the dead, small and great, standing before God, and books were opened. And another book was opened, which is the Book of Life. And the dead were judged according to their works, by the things which were written in the books. The sea gave up the dead who were in it, and Death and Hades delivered up the dead who were in them. And they were judged, each one according to his works. Then Death and Hades were cast into the lake of fire. This is the second death. And anyone not found written in the Book of Life was cast into the lake of fire" (vv. 12–15).

You can rejoice because your name is written in the Book of Life.

God's Secret Formula Is Joy

Joy doesn't depend on how much money you've got. Joy doesn't depend upon whether you don't have any storms in life. Joy doesn't depend upon what happens to you and your family. Joy does not give way to heartache and pain. Joy is knowing your name is written in heaven and Jesus is your Lord. So rejoice!

And what the world needs is joy. Joy will sustain you when the winds are blowing. Joy will sustain you when it's dark. Joy will sustain you when you get a bad report from the doctor. Joy will sustain you in the battles of life. And the reason we can rejoice is because our names have been enrolled as the sons and daughters of the Most High God. Let heaven shout it and earth send it back with joy. Our names are written in the Lamb's Book of Life, and we are tapped into the abundant life of God.

Joy—God's secret formula.
Joy—stamina that keeps you going.
Joy—because we see what the world doesn't see.
Joy—because we know what the world doesn't know.
Joy—because our ears hear what the world can't hear.

If you know your name is written in the Lamb's Book of Life, you can have that joy because everything is settled in life and in death. When you realize what you've done, and your name is written there in letters of gold, no matter what happens to you, you've got it made, because you're headed for an eternity where there's no death, no sighing, no crying, no pain, no separation, no sorrow; where you'll be happy forever and forever. If we don't see you here, we'll see you over there.

So if you have trouble and trials and tribulations, get joyful about it. Start thinking about how great your God is. Start thinking about the greater One who lives on the inside of you. Recognize that whatever heartache may have come to pass, it didn't come to stay. Joy unspeakable and full of glory is in Christ!

You just have to face the fact that you've got a decision to make. When the trouble gets bigger, turn up the joy valve. Do a little dance. Glory in your God. Just praise Him more and more. Let your joy come out, not because it's in the natural that you should be joyous; but you know something that the world doesn't know. You hear something that the world doesn't hear.

That joy is God's secret formula. That joy will get you through any trial, any storm, over any mountain, and through any tunnel of pain. Oh, you may be hurting in your body, but your spirit is singing. That is joy.

You know how it's going to come out. Your name is written in the Lamb's Book of Life. Jesus is your Lord. God is your Father. The Holy Spirit dwells in you. Angels are all around you, and goodness and mercy are following you.

Joy unspeakable AND FULL OF GLORY IS IN CHRIST!

Reflections from
JOEL

*T*he apostle Paul wrote many of his letters while incarcerated, often in prison cells not much bigger than a small bathroom. Some historians and Bible commentators believe that the raw sewage system of that day ran right through one of the dungeons in which he was imprisoned. Yet Paul wrote such amazing faith-filled words as, "Rejoice in the Lord always. Again I will say, rejoice!" (Philippians 4:4). Notice that we are to rejoice and be joyful at all times. In your difficulties, when things aren't going your way, make a decision to stay full of joy.

You need to understand that the enemy is not really after your dreams, your health, or your finances. He's after your joy. The Bible says that "the joy of the LORD is your strength" (Nehemiah 8:10), and your enemy knows if he can deceive you into living down in the dumps and depressed, you are not going to have the necessary strength—physically, emotionally, or spiritually—to withstand his attacks.

When you rejoice in the midst of your difficulties, you're giving the enemy a black eye. He doesn't know what to do with people who keep giving God praise despite their circumstances. Learn how to smile and laugh. Quit being so uptight and stressed out. Make your choice to enjoy your life to the fullest today.

CHAPTER FIVE

An Abundance *of* Provision *for* Your Every Lack

If we want to live our lives in the abundance of God, we must have a faith that doesn't limit God. I realize there are people who say that no one can limit God, but that's not what I find in His Word or in my personal experience.

In Psalm 78, the psalmist recounts God's miraculous deliverance of the people of Israel from Egypt. Yet even after they had crossed the Red Sea on dry ground, the people "spoke against God: They said, 'Can God prepare a table in the wilderness? Behold, He struck the rock, so that the waters gushed out, and the streams overflowed.

Can He give bread also? Can He provide meat for His people?' Therefore the LORD heard this and was furious; so a fire was kindled against Jacob, and anger also came up against Israel, because they did not believe in God, and did not trust in His salvation. Yet He had commanded the clouds above, and opened the doors of heaven, had rained down manna on them to eat, and given them of the bread of heaven. Men ate angels' food; He sent them food to the full. He caused an east wind to blow in the heavens; and by His power He brought in the south wind. He also rained meat on them like the dust, feathered fowl like the sand of the seas; and He let them fall in the midst of their camp, all around their dwellings. So they ate and were well filled, for He gave them their own desire" (vv. 19–29).

Verses 40–42 reveal the heart of the problem: "How often they provoked Him in the wilderness, and grieved Him in the desert! Yes, again and again *they tempted God, and limited the Holy One of Israel.* They did not remember His power: the day when He redeemed them from the enemy."

Have a faith that doesn't limit God.

DON'T LIMIT GOD THROUGH DOUBT, UNBELIEF, AND IGNORANCE

As remarkable as this story is, and as often as we wonder how the Israelites could act this way, the truth is that we tend to do the same. In bringing us to faith in Christ, God has given us great miracles and mighty deliverances, but as we travel our way through our own wildernesses, we sometimes get a little weary and forget what God has done. It is easy to begin to limit God and say, "Well, God helped me last year, but I wonder if He's getting tired of helping me."

We can limit God through our unbelief and doubts. When Peter saw Jesus walking on the water, he said, "Lord, if it is You, command me to come to You on the water" (Matthew 14:28). And the Bible says that Peter did indeed step out of the boat and walk on the water. We tend to focus on Peter sinking in the water, but the Bible emphasizes that he truly did walk on the water. It was not until Peter looked about him at the boisterous wind and the waves that he began to sink.

"And immediately Jesus stretched out His hand and caught him, and said to him, 'O you of little faith, why did you doubt?'" (Matthew 14:31). See, *doubt sinks you. Faith holds you up.*

When you look around at your circumstances and see all the things that are coming against you, and everything that could happen to you, and everything that the enemy tells you is going to happen to you, you begin to sink. But when you keep your eyes on Jesus, you keep walking on the water.

We limit God by doubting Him. We limit God by our unbelief. And we can limit God by our ignorance.

Faith begins where knowledge is. If we do not know that God is a miracle-working God, that limits God. If we do not know that God heals the sick, that limits God. If we do not know that God can provide for our every need, that limits God. We must have knowledge of the Word of God.

According to Psalm 78, the people of Israel were so obstinate in their unbelief that they made God angry. God had delivered them through the Red Sea and by the power of miracles brought them out of Egypt. With their own eyes they had witnessed phenomenal deliverances from God. Yet when they got into the desert, they began to complain. They said, "Can God take care of us in this wilderness? What about our children? How are we going to get clothes for them? What about our own bodies? What are we going to eat?" They questioned whether God could provide them with "a table in the wilderness."

One provocation came after another, and finally God became "furious" with them. They said, "What are we going to do? Can God, this God who brought us out of Egypt, can He furnish food and clothes out here in the middle of the desert?" The Bible states they limited the Holy One of Israel.

If we do not know that God can provide for our every need, that limits God.

In response, God said, "I'll show you what I can do. Moses, strike the rock, and it'll give forth water," and it did. And then He said, "I'll show you how you'll eat," and He rained manna down for forty years. When they cried out for meat, He brought the south and east winds together and rained down so many birds upon them that they ate until it came out of their nostrils.

God said, "Don't ever say, 'Can God?'" Rather, you should shout, "God can!"

I don't know what you face today. I do not know what needs you have; but don't limit God by ignorance, doubt, and unbelief. We have a great God. He made the world. He flung the stars from His fingertips. He keeps everything in order by the word of

His mighty power. He is the great I Am, and He's a God of love and mercy who wants to provide for all of your needs. So don't limit God.

Don't Limit God by Your Mind, Finances, or Job

You can limit God by your mind. Sometimes we face life's challenges and are determined to figure it all out on our own. We think, *What in the world am I going to do? What in the world could God do for me? I'm all on my own on this, and nobody's going to help me.* You get your mind all worked up, but it's the carnal mind, which is enmity against God (Romans 8:7). Your carnal mind can't see a way out, but our minds are finite. God is bigger than our minds.

Whenever I think about living in the abundance of God, I think of Casey, who was a house mover down in Beaumont, Texas, and a street evangelist for Jesus. One day he and all his men went way out in the country to move a building. Some of the men in his crew thought he was out of his mind because he was always talking about miracles. When he got way out in the country, he pulled off on the shoulder of the highway and said, "You know what, I've forgotten my chain. I have to have a chain to do this job."

Because Casey was always talking about miracles, some of the men snickered and laughed and made fun of him behind his back, wondering what he was going to do to get a chain. Then Casey said, "Come up here, men. Let's pray for a chain." They thought Casey was a nut case, praying for a chain. *Would God drop one out of heaven?*

But Casey refused to limit God by his mind. When you walk with God, you know He can and will do anything to bring glory to His Name. So out there on the shoulder of the highway, Casey lifted his hands and began to pray, "Oh, Lord Jesus, You know I forgot my chain. I'm sorry, but I forgot it, and I have to have a chain. We're too far out here in the country to get a chain, and I don't have time to go back to get one. God, I need a chain. Oh, God, in the Name of Jesus, give me a chain."

Who would pray like that? How would God give Casey a chain in the middle of nowhere? But as he was praying in the midst of his crew's unbelief, a pickup truck came down the highway going really fast and turned right. As it turned, out of the back end of the truck rolled a chain, and it came to rest curled up right at Casey's feet!

Don't limit God. God is able to do exceeding abundantly above all that you ask or think.

Don't limit God by your finances either, for God is able to increase your finances. You say, "Well, I want to do something for the world. I want to do something for my family." Don't limit God by your paycheck. Don't limit God by your job. God is bigger than your checkbook and your job.

Don't Limit God by Your Circumstances

Don't limit God by your circumstances. In 2 Chronicles 20, King Jehoshaphat looked out his window in Jerusalem one day, and three great armies were coming against him. As far as their circumstances were concerned, the king and people of Jerusalem and Judah were doomed. Perhaps that's the way your circumstances present themselves today. You may have so many unsolvable problems around you that you just don't know what in the world you're going to do. Well, you're in the place of Jehoshaphat, which is a good place to be, as long as you don't limit God by your circumstances.

So Jehoshaphat gathered all the women and children and the men out in the field, and they lifted up their voice to God. Jehoshaphat said, "O Lord God of our fathers, are You not God in heaven, and do You not rule over all the kingdoms of the nations, and in Your hand is there not power and might, so that no one is able to withstand You? . . . O our God, will You not judge them? For we have no power against this great multitude that is coming against us; nor do we know what to do, but our eyes are upon You" (vv. 6, 12).

They believed that God could get them out of that impossible situation. And the Bible says: "Then the Spirit of the LORD came upon Jahaziel . . . And he said, 'Listen, all you of Judah and you inhabitants of Jerusalem, and you, King Jehoshaphat! Thus says the LORD to you: 'Do not be afraid nor dismayed because of this great multitude, for the battle is not yours, but God's. . . . You will not need to fight in this battle. Position yourselves, stand still and see the salvation of the LORD, who is with you, O Judah and Jerusalem!'" (vv. 14–15, 17).

When the army of Israel went out the next morning, they sent singers out in front of the army, saying, "Praise the LORD, for His mercy endures forever." They did not need to resort to stealth and secrecy or attack from every direction. They put the praisers out in front of their army, for the joy of the Lord is our strength. And the enemy heard it, became frightened, and was defeated without the people of Judah lifting a sword, yet taking all the spoil.

People may be coming against you today. Everything may be rising up against you. You don't know what to do.

Cry out to God. Don't limit God. He is able to deliver by many or by few. With God, all things are possible!

Don't Limit God by Your Medical Report

Don't limit God by your doctor's report. We thank God for doctors and medication. But remember that at times they are limited in what they can do to help people. My son Paul, who is a surgeon, once told me that I should not call Jesus a doctor. I asked him, "Why not? He healed people." My son said, "Because doctors, when they hear you say that, know how limited they are. They know they have to look some people in the face and say, 'I've done all I can do. I can't do any more.' Jesus is more than a doctor. He is a Healer."

Don't be discourteous to a doctor, but don't limit yourself to their report. They're telling you as much as the technology shows and as much as they know from their training and experience. But there's another report above and beyond the report of the doctor. The doctor's diagnosis told us that Dodie, my wife, was going to die in 1981. Her doctor looked into my face and said, "Your wife will be dead within a few weeks, Pastor—not months, weeks. She has metastatic cancer of the liver. We know nothing to do for her. Make up your mind. She's going to be dead in a few weeks."

I looked at him, and I said, "Doctor, we believe in miracles." He looked at me and said sternly, "You're going to have to have one." I looked back at him and said, "We'll get one." That was over thirty years ago. God healed her. She is a walking miracle. Don't limit God.

BELIEVING GOD CHANGES EVERYTHING

What if, when the angel came to Mary, the blessed virgin, she had limited God. The angel Gabriel came and said, "Rejoice, highly favored one, the Lord is with you; blessed are you among women! . . . And behold, you will conceive in your womb and bring forth a Son, and shall call His name Jesus. He will be great, and will be called the Son of the Highest; and the Lord God will give Him the throne of His father David. And He will reign over the house of Jacob forever, and of His kingdom there will be no end" (Luke 1:28, 31–33).

One can easily understand Mary's response: "How can this be, since I do not know a man?" (v. 34). To which, the angel answered, "The Holy Spirit will come upon you, and the power of the Highest will overshadow you; therefore, also, that Holy One who is to be born will be called the Son of God" (v. 35).

What if Mary had said, "Now, look, Gabriel, you look bright and beautiful and full of authority. But this has never been done before, and I don't know anybody else who ever had a message like this. You realize I'm going to be accused of having an affair with a man and going around here pregnant not even being married. Why are you trying to get me into trouble? Wherever you came from, go on back."

This word from the angel Gabriel was not natural; it was supernatural. She could have doubted him, but thank God she didn't. Thank God, she received the seed of God, the Word of God into her womb, and Jesus was born, and now He is our Savior and our Lord!

What if Moses' parents had limited God when the Egyptians were killing the newborn Jewish boys? Baby Moses was so beautiful, and they could see destiny written on his face. What if they had said, "Well, it's no use. He's going to be killed like all the rest of the babies." But they didn't limit God. They said, "God, we're going to trust You." They took creative steps to save their child, hiding him away in a little basket down in the Nile. Not only was Moses not killed, but God found a way to get him right into the heart of Pharaoh's palace through Pharaoh's daughter. She took him for her own child and raised him as a prince in Egypt, and he became the mighty deliverer of the Jewish nation.

GOD WILL MEET YOUR EVERY NEED

So many people look at their lives and only see the addiction to drugs or alcohol or pornography or the financial mess they've gotten themselves in, and they say, "What am I going to do? Even God can't help me." Don't limit God.

Consider the demoniac who said his name was Legion in Mark 5. A legion was 6,000, and there was a legion of demons inside of him. The Bible states that he could break apart shackles and chains and that he was crying out and cutting himself with stones. He slept in the graveyard among the dead, and all the people in the countryside knew he was there. They didn't believe that anything, including God, could help him. Nobody ever came to him with help. Nobody ever said to him, "The God of Abraham, Isaac, and Jacob can help you." No, he was a lost cause. They limited God.

Throw away your doubt and your unbelief today and put your faith in God through the Lord Jesus Christ.

But one day Jesus got in a boat and came to the country of the Gadarenes, and that man with 6,000 demons came running to Him and fell at His feet in worship. Jesus delivered him of those demons. And the once hopeless man sat at the feet of Jesus, clothed and in his right mind!

When Jesus got ready to go, the man begged that he might go with Jesus. But Jesus said, "No. You go to your family and friends and begin to publicize what God has done for you." And when the man went back home and began to say, "Jesus healed me. Jesus delivered me. Jesus saved me," he was an example of what happens when you don't limit God.

What is your circumstance today? Where are you today? Are you discouraged? Are you downcast? Does it look as though no one can or ever will help you? Does it look like there's no help on any side wherever you look? Well, stop looking around you and instead look up. God is able to do exceeding abundantly above all you can ask or think.

Don't limit God. Throw away your doubt and your unbelief today and put your faith in God through the Lord Jesus Christ. He can provide for whatever you need. Simply trust Him!

Reflections from
JOEL

*W*hat does God have in store for you today? His dream for your life is so much greater than you can imagine. If God showed you everything He has in store for you, it would boggle your mind.

Many people miss pivotal opportunities in their lives because they've grown accustomed to the status quo. They refuse to make room in their own thinking for the new things God wants to do in their lives. When a great opportunity comes along, rather than launching out in faith, they say, "Well, that could never happen to me. That's just too good to be true."

It's time to quit limiting God. Remember: God is your source, and His creativity and resources are unlimited! God may give you a dream or an idea for an invention, a book, a song, or a movie. One idea from God can forever change the course of your life. God is not limited by what you have or don't have. He can do anything, if you will simply stop limiting Him in your thinking.

CHAPTER SIX

An Abundance
of Love
to Reach Out
to Others

To live in the abundance of God is to live as Jesus lived. One of the beautiful dimensions about the life of Jesus is expressed clearly in Matthew 14:14: "And when Jesus went out He saw a great multitude; and He was moved with compassion for them, and healed their sick." If we miss out on the heart of Jesus for others, we will miss the abundant life He has for us.

What moved Jesus? It was divine compassion rising up in His heart. He felt the divine flow of love flowing out of His spirit. Which way did it flow? It flowed toward the multitudes. When it flowed toward the multitudes, Jesus followed the flow of compassionate love and helped the hurting, sick, fallen, and those tormented by Satan. The end result was that the healing love of God brought deliverance to the suffering people of that day.

Compassion moved Jesus. Love directed His life. It led Him constantly.

The divine flow of God's love can move you toward the people God wants to reach. We need to watch for the rising of this supernatural love in our hearts and be ready to follow wherever it flows.

One of the most remarkable scriptures in God's Word is found in 2 John 6: "And what this love consists in is this: that we live and walk in accordance with and guided by His commandments (His orders, ordinances, precepts, teaching). This is the commandment, as you have heard from the beginning, that you continue to walk in love [guided by it and following it]" (AMP).

In this verse is found a powerful life principle: *continue to walk in love [guided by it and following it].* Nothing in all my experience as a Christian, apart from the baptism of the Holy Spirit, has proved richer or more profitable to me personally than the spiritual truth of the power inherent in the divine flow of love.

God Is Love

Another scripture that I find very helpful is this: "And we know (understand, recognize, are conscious of, by observation and by experience) and believe (adhere to and put faith in and rely on) the love God cherishes for us. God is love, and he who dwells and continues in love dwells and continues in God, and God dwells and continues in him. In this [union and communion with Him] love is brought to completion and attains perfection with us, that we may have confidence for the day of judgment [with assurance and boldness to face Him], because as He is, so are we in this world. There is no fear in love [dread does not exist], but full-grown (complete, perfect) love turns fear out of doors and expels every trace of terror! For fear brings with it the thought of punishment, and [so] he who is afraid has not reached the full maturity of love [is not yet grown into love's complete perfection]" (1 John 4:16–18 AMP).

Love goes to the door, opens it, and commands, "Fear, you go out!"

This doesn't mean you are not a Christian if you have anxieties and fears. It just means that you need to grow a little bit more and learn more of God's Word.

"We love Him because He first loved us" (1 John 4:19).

God is a great big wonderful God. We cannot put Him in a corner and say, "This is all there is to God." There are so many scintillating, marvelous rays of the divine personality that we could never capture them all. But one of the richest is this: God is love.

There are two forces in the world—fear and love.

Dread, terror, and fear bring sickness, sorrow, trouble, and anxiety.

On the other hand, there is the kingdom of love. This flow of love brings life, health, and peace.

The enemy would make us believe that the burden of dread and fear that he places on the human heart is sent from God. He tries to make us think that we are trembling at the voice of God, when all the time he is the one who is causing our anxiety.

Some people say, "I can't understand the difference between the voice of God and the voice of the enemy." There are some areas where this may be true in a sense, but usually you will find it is the enemy who brings fear, and it is God who brings love.

I never become frightened when my wife says to me, "Darling, I love you." This doesn't disturb me. It doesn't make me tremble or run to a counselor and say, "I am disturbed because my wife says she loves me." That would be foolishness. It brings comfort and joy to my heart to know that my wife loves me.

Love doesn't bring fear and torment. Satan does!

When the enemy comes along with his bag of fear, we shake and tremble. "I was afraid" was the excuse of the man who buried his talent in the earth (Matthew 25). Fear caused him to bury his talent rather than use it.

God is not the author of such fear. *God is love!*

There is a way in which we should fear God, and this kind of fear is more than just reverence, which is the way we usually think of fearing God. When God tells us to do something, we must do it. Otherwise, we will have to accept the consequences of disobedience to His commands.

There is no fear in love, but full-grown love turns fear out of doors and expels every trace of terror!

As for me, I am not going to fool around with God, because there have been times when I've had to learn the hard way. God will put you through one of His grades in the school of life, and you'll be sure to graduate, because you won't want to go through that a second time!

God loves those who tremble at His Word. We should be ready to listen to Him.

But this is a different kind of reverence and fear. The fear that the enemy brings has torment.

The deepest desire of my heart is that I might please Him who counted me worthy to be called into His service and to be a useful instrument in His hands. But even greater than my desire to be used by God is His desire to use me. He wants us all to be fruitful Christians, and He wants to help us be fruitful.

The Divine Flow of Love

Some people say to me, "I would like to feel God." When they say this, they are usually thinking of some sort of emotional or physical sensation. They want to feel something like an electric current surging through their body as evidence that God is with them. Or they want an experience such as they may have heard about from someone else—fire out of heaven, flashes of lightning, or a bright light shining down from heaven. They think that is the only way to feel God. But that is not the only way. We can feel God's presence and power in many ways.

God is love. There is a way of feeling God by feeling love. When "the love of God has been poured out in our hearts by the Holy Spirit who was given to us" (Romans 5:5), we are feeling God.

There can come into our lives a flow of divine love and compassion that has nothing to do with our minds. It has nothing to do with our personalities. It is implanted instantaneously and supernaturally in our hearts and rises up in us. Then it flows out of us toward individuals. This is surely the moving of God. When you feel this love, you are feeling God, for God is love.

I remember the first time I felt this divine flow of love—this surging of God's power. Shortly after I received the baptism of the Holy Spirit, I told my congregation that God is a miracle worker and that I was praying for miracles to take place in our church. However, it didn't happen, and I cried to the Lord, "Why don't you confirm your Word, Lord?" I learned that there is a vast difference in telling people that and in preaching the Word of God. The Bible says that the disciples "went out and preached everywhere, the Lord working with them and confirming the word through the accompanying signs" (Mark 16:20). God has not obligated Himself to confirm what I say. He has obligated Himself to confirm what He has said.

The Lord showed this to me and spoke to my heart, "Son, go out on that platform and preach My Word, and I will confirm my Word. I will stand behind My Word."

I began to do this. Sunday after Sunday, I faithfully preached the Word. Then one Wednesday night God seemed to give me a special anointing, and the scriptures became alive as the words poured from my heart to the congregation. As I began to talk about the Jesus of the Bible, it seemed as though He marched right out of the scriptures from the Gospels and stood in our midst.

Faith began to rise. Suddenly I noticed a girl about twelve or thirteen years of age sitting in the front of the church. She had a clubbed foot and had to wear a special built-up shoe. Her ankle was as stiff as steel. I felt a divine flow of love in my heart streaming out toward this girl. Something welled up in me like a golden bowl full of love. I didn't think about her being sick or crippled. It was not so much that I was conscious of her being in need of healing. I felt only a supernatural kind of compassion for her. This love just poured out of me, and I felt as if I wanted to go to her and pick her up in my arms.

It was that night, without my even laying hands upon her, that suddenly, as she looked to Jesus, her ankle instantly became normal. A miracle of God took place as a result of the divine flow of love to her.

If you wonder why it happened, know simply that it was God!

FOLLOW LOVE. BE GUIDED BY LOVE.

God is love, and he who feels love feels God.

The scripture in 2 John 6 states to "continue to walk in love [guided by it and following it]" (AMP).

Do you want to follow God? Then follow love.

Do you want to be guided by the Holy Spirit? Then be guided by love.

Wherever that stream of love flows out, follow it.

Many times over the years I have had it stream out of me toward others, both those near and those far away. I have picked up the phone and called them. If I had been completely honest with them, I would have said, "Friend, there is a stream of love flowing out of me toward you." But usually I don't tell them this. I just minister to them on the thing that is on my heart, and I do it in the Name of the Lord Jesus.

God mends hearts. He encourages lives. He works miracles by His love.

Follow love! Be guided by love!

If you wonder, *Where is God? Where is He leading me? To whom does He want me to minister? How will I know?*

Wherever that stream of love flows out,
FOLLOW IT.

God is love. Follow love. Be guided by love.

I once heard Oral Roberts tell of the time when he was called to the hospital to minister to the sick baby of one of the employees who worked for him. The child was very near death and had been placed under an oxygen tent. No visitors were allowed; however, Roberts was permitted to go into the room. He could not lift up the oxygen tent to lay hands on the baby and pray for him, so he just reached a finger under the corner of the tent and touched its tiny foot.

As Roberts stood there for what seemed a long time, he felt something wash through him and into the child. God's love was flowing through him to the baby. The next morning the child was well on its way to recovery!

God is love.

If you have received Jesus as your personal Savior, you have had the love of God shed abroad in your heart by the Holy Spirit. If you have been baptized in the Holy Spirit, that love flows out far more freely.

Let me urge you never to follow hate. Never follow evil thoughts or an impulse to get even. Never return evil for evil. Never follow that which is selfish or that which is full of greed and covetousness. These are not of God.

Follow the divine flow of love. Be guided by it every day.

I am certain that at some time or another you have felt this divine love. Have you ever been cooking dinner or working on the job, when suddenly you get a thought of someone with love and tenderness? Have you thought, *God bless her. I would love to see her right now and give her a big hug and encourage her.*

Follow that impulse. That is God. Don't miss the blessing. You are experiencing God. Be guided by love.

Where is it? It is streaming over to that person's house. Get in your car and follow that stream as quickly as you can. Minister to the person while God is still moving in your heart. This person needs God's miracle power!

WALK IN THE HOLY SPIRIT

God's love is not going to flow in us if we are selfish and mean. God's love is not going to flow in us if we are covetous, or if we fuss and argue. You cannot harbor bitterness and ill will. You can't let ugly feelings linger in your heart and still feel this divine flow of love that I am talking about. Let us keep our hearts clean of all animosity toward anyone. Let us be willing to humble ourselves, not to have a high opinion of ourselves, but be willing to make peace with everybody. Then the love of God will dwell in our hearts.

The dove is a symbol of the Holy Spirit. The gentle dove of the Holy Spirit is not going to abide and shed abroad the love of God if we have animosity and unforgiveness in our hearts.

You might wonder, *Where shall I go today?* Get full of love and see where it goes out. You don't have to manufacture it. When this divine flow of love comes, you automatically begin to think of others. Stay full of the Holy Spirit. Suddenly you will have somebody on your heart. Until then, just go on, love God and do your work. Then when you feel God's love flowing through you to a certain person, act right then. Don't hesitate. Pick up the phone and call them right then. Go to them personally, if possible.

When the Lord moves on me in this way, flooding in my heart with His supernatural love for an individual, I pick up the phone and call them. I say, "Well, I don't know what your need is (unless God has revealed it to me), but God has impressed me that He is going to bless you today and that His love is flowing out toward you. Whatever you have need of, you are going to get it because God's love is shining on your heart. God guided me to you today to minister to you in the Name of the Lord Jesus."

Many times these people have broken into tears and said, "Oh, you will never know the burden I've been under!" But God knew.

Too many times we try to make it such a complicated thing. But it is not. God is love! Follow love! Be guided by love!

Walk in the stream of God's love. Be guided by it and follow it; for where love is streaming, God is going and God is working.

Don't miss out on this precious experience by holding back when God moves on you and by failing to yield to Him when He leads you to reach out and touch and bless the lives of others.

Whatever you have need of,
YOU ARE GOING TO GET IT
because God's love is shining on your heart.

Do Not Complicate Divine Love

God is love. He who follows love follows God, and he who is guided by love is guided by God.

You may say, "That sounds so simple." It is!

The apostle Paul said, "But earnestly desire and zealously cultivate the greatest and best gifts and graces (the higher gifts and the choicest graces). And yet I will show you a still more excellent way [one that is better by far and the highest of them all—love]" (1 Corinthians 12:31 AMP). Then Paul said in the next chapter, "Though I speak with the tongues of men and of angels, but have not love, I have become sounding brass or a clanging cymbal. And though I have the gift of prophecy, and understand all mysteries and all knowledge, and though I have all faith, so that I could remove mountains, but have not love, I am nothing" (1 Corinthians 13:1–2). Paul was saying that even though we may speak with tongues, even though we may have the gifts of the Spirit operating in our lives, if we do all these things and have not love, they are worth nothing.

Further in this same chapter, Paul said, "Love suffers long and is kind; love does not envy; love does not parade itself, is not puffed up; does not behave rudely, does not seek its own, is not provoked, thinks no evil; does not rejoice in iniquity, but rejoices in the truth" (1 Corinthians 13:4–6).

You can have everything in the world, including all the knowledge that the finest universities can give you, but if your heart is not full of love, it is not going to amount to anything. But if you will be guided by love, you can experience some of God's richest blessings in your life.

Success in Christian living is rooted in love.

First of all, you have to get full of love. Allow the love of God to be shed abroad in your heart by the Holy Spirit every day. Walk in love, be guided by it, and follow it.

Success in Christian living is rooted in love. The fruit of the Spirit is, first of all, love (Galatians 5:22). When you feel the glorious love of God, you are feeling the Holy Spirit. As you follow that love, you and the Lord will be working together.

Get rid of any bitterness that may be in your heart. Avoid strife and bitterness. Never allow any filthy talk to come from your lips. Stay right with God and live peaceably with others. When someone wrongs you, forgive him instantly, as you will not harbor any grudge. Rid your heart of anything that would be displeasing to the Lord and stay humble before Him.

With pure motives of heart, you can stay full of compassion as you let God fill your heart every day with His divine love.

Then, when you are least expecting it, someone will enter your mind and you will feel impressed to call them or go see them. Or it may be that you will just be sitting next to them in a church service. This has happened to me. I have sometimes been sitting in an audience when, suddenly as I looked at individuals, God's love flowed out of me toward them.

Let me say it again. God is love! When you feel this divine flow of love, you are feeling God! Be guided by this divine love! Follow it! It will lead you to the person God wants you to help. When you get there, God will be there waiting to confirm His Word and bring deliverance.

From this day forth, life will be the most exciting for you!

You will enjoy the new adventures awaiting you as you follow the divine flow of love!

Reflections from JOEL

We're all so busy. We have our own priorities and important plans and agendas. Often, our attitude is: I don't want to be inconvenienced. Don't bother me with your problems. I've got enough problems of my own. Too often, because of our own selfishness, we choose to close our hearts to others.

If you want to experience God's abundant life, you must start taking time to help other people. Sometimes if we would just take the time to listen to people, we could help initiate a healing process in their lives. So many people have pain bottled up inside them. They have nobody they can talk to; they don't trust anybody. If you can open your heart of compassion and be that person's friend—without judging or condemning—and simply have an ear to listen, you may help lift that heavy burden.

You will be amazed at what a positive impact you can have if you will just learn to be a good listener. Learn to follow the flow of God's divine love.

CHAPTER SEVEN

An Abundance *of* Power *for* Your Weakness

Humility is the secret to continually living in the abundance of God as well as the secret to usefulness in the kingdom of God. We can truly reign in life as kings through the power of humility.

God greatly rewards the man or woman who lives a life of humility. "By humility and the fear of the LORD are riches and honor and life" (Proverbs 22:4).

Humility is not weakness. It is a total lack of confidence in your own ability and a total dependence on God's ability.

All Christians should learn to walk in the spirit of humility. It is a very important attitude, and the Word of God has much to say about it: "I therefore, the prisoner for the Lord, appeal to and beg you to walk (lead a life) worthy of the [divine] calling to which you have been called [with behavior that is a credit to the summons to God's service, living as becomes you] with complete lowliness of mind (humility) and meekness (unselfishness, gentleness, mildness), with patience, bearing with one another and making allowances because you love one another" (Ephesians 4:1–2 AMP).

Many people are used by God for a short period of time, but humility is the key to continual usefulness. Paul warned the believers in Rome: "For by the grace (unmerited favor of God) given to me I warn everyone among you not to estimate and think of himself more highly than he ought [not to have an exaggerated opinion of his own importance], but to rate his ability with sober judgment, each according to the degree of faith apportioned by God to him" (Romans 12:3 AMP). We must realize that all blessings come from God. All that we are, and all that we have, is the result of the grace of God in our lives.

I am continually aware of the fact that the good that is done in Lakewood Church is a result of the work of the Holy Spirit. God saved me at the age of seventeen when I was selling popcorn in a theater. It is only by the grace of God that I am able to minister to others.

Pride and an exaggerated opinion of yourself will cut off your usefulness. You may think, *Well, they do not have the respect for me that they should have! After all, I'm somebody!* That is an exaggerated opinion of your importance.

I realize that the only authority that I have as a pastor is a spiritual, intangible authority that Jesus gives me. If He withdraws that authority, I have absolutely nothing.

OUR SUFFICIENCY IS FROM GOD ALONE

God set many ministries in the church. We should always hold one another in high esteem because God has a special work for each of us. Every ministry, according to Romans 12:4–8, is important.

Learn to walk
in the spirit of humility.

For as we have many members in one body, but all the members do not have the same function, so we, being many, are one body in Christ, and individually members of one another. Having then gifts differing according to the grace that is given to us, let us use them:

> *if prophecy, let us prophesy in proportion*
> *to our faith;*
> *or ministry, let us use it in our ministering;*
> *he who teaches, in teaching;*
> *he who exhorts, in exhortation;*
> *he who gives, with liberality;*
> *he who leads, with diligence;*
> *he who shows mercy, with cheerfulness.*

Our responsibility is to function in the ministry that God has given us. Not every person is called into one of the five-fold ministries. God is using lay people all over the world in supernatural ways. Every ministry is necessary for the perfecting and full equipping of the saints.

We need to give unqualified courtesy to every person. We should never treat anyone disrespectfully. "But He gives more grace. Therefore He says: 'God resists the proud, but gives grace to the humble'" (James 4:6).

Pride destroys the flow of the abundance of God in our lives. God resists the proud. He does not just resist proud laymen; He resists proud preachers. He resists proud wives. God resists the proud and gives grace to the humble.

We all need the grace of God in our lives!

The apostle Paul had a beautiful spirit of humility. He said, "I can do all things through Christ who strengthens me" (Philippians 4:13). Again Paul confessed, "Yet in all these things we are more than conquerors through Him who loved us" (Romans 8:37). Paul spoke of the mighty works that he could do through Jesus. Our confession should be what we have in Christ, and not what we can do in our own power and ability.

In his silent moments of reflection, Paul, remembering what a mess he made of his life before he knew Jesus, said, "I am the least of the apostles, who am not worthy to be called an apostle, because I persecuted the church of God" (1 Corinthians 15:9). Paul was a man who knew within himself that he was not worthy of the least of the mercies of God, yet he knew who he was in Jesus. That is a man who can shake nations!

"Not that we are sufficient of ourselves to think of anything as being from ourselves, but our sufficiency is from God" (2 Corinthians 3:5). What good thing do we have that we have not received from God? He is our sufficiency. He is our source of life.

Humility is the key to living in the abundance of God and being continually useful in the kingdom of God.

The Humblest Man on the Earth

The Bible says of the life of Moses: "Now the man Moses was very humble, more than all men who were on the face of the earth" (Numbers 12:3). Moses was the most humble man on the face of the earth, and God used him in a mighty way.

Many people think Moses was ignorant because of his humility, but in the New Testament, Stephen spoke very highly of him by inspiration of the Holy Spirit: "And Moses was learned in all the wisdom of the Egyptians, and was mighty in words and deeds" (Acts 7:22). Egypt was the greatest and most advanced nation of Moses' day. Moses had all the privileges of its universities. He was a mighty orator, and the Bible says that he was mighty in deeds.

God revealed to Moses that he would be the deliverer of the children of Israel, but he was not yet ready. In all his pride, Moses slew an Egyptian who was fighting with a fellow Hebrew. He thought the children of Israel would understand that he was chosen to be their deliverer (Acts 7:23–25).

Moses felt he was well able to deliver the Israelites from their bondage in Egypt. He had the ability to speak and do great works. He was ready to do the job. He probably even felt that God had chosen him because of his great abilities!

Moses was a proud man. He felt he was sufficient, but he was not. He had the call of God upon his life, but he was not ready for God to trust him with that task.

Forty years later, on the backside of the desert, Moses had still not fulfilled the call of God. He felt defeated, but God appeared to him in a burning bush and spoke to him: "Come now, therefore, and I will send you to Pharaoh that you may bring My people, the children of Israel, out of Egypt. But Moses said to God, 'Who am I that I should go to Pharaoh, and that I should bring the children of Israel out of Egypt?'" (Exodus 3:10–11).

The first words that Moses spoke were, "Who am I?" Forty years before he had thought, *Here I am! I am God's great deliverer!* Here is a man who had all the skills and learning of the Egyptians and was mighty in word, yet Moses argues, "O my Lord, I am not eloquent, neither before nor since You have spoken to Your servant; but I am slow of speech and slow of tongue" (Exodus 4:10). Was Moses lying? No! He finally realized that without God he was nothing. Only by the power of God could he bring deliverance to the children of Israel.

God had to show Moses that he could depend on the power of God. "Then Moses answered and said, 'But suppose they will not believe me or listen to my voice; suppose they say, "The LORD has not appeared to you."' So the LORD said to him, 'What is that in your hand?' He said, 'A rod.' And He said, 'Cast it on the ground.' So he cast it on the ground, and it became a serpent; and Moses fled from it. Then the LORD said to Moses, 'Reach out your hand and take it by the tail' (and he reached out his hand and caught it, and it became a rod in his hand), 'that they may believe that the LORD God of their fathers, the God of Abraham, the God of Isaac, and the God of Jacob, has appeared to you'" (Exodus 4:1–5).

Moses later marched out of Egypt with two million slaves, waving the rod of God in his hand. This time, God was with him. Moses learned to reign in life through the spirit of humility.

IT IS NOT ABOUT YOU; IT IS ABOUT GOD

God uses and exalts many men and women. Unfortunately, some believers get a touch of the blessing of God, and then they become proud and haughty. That is a dangerous place to be in.

Oral Robert once said, "The most dangerous time in a man's life is when he feels so sufficient that he does not need faith in God."

The most dangerous place is that secure place where you think you have it made. You have all the money you need. You have no challenges. You have no need to trust God and His power.

I encourage you to forever extend yourself to the place where God must work for you.

Moses chose to humble himself, and God blessed him mightily, but soon criticism came from the mouths of his own brother and sister. "Then Miriam and Aaron spoke against Moses because of the Ethiopian woman whom he had married; for he had married an Ethiopian woman. So they said, 'Has the LORD indeed spoken only through Moses? Has He not spoken through us also?' And the Lord heard it" (Numbers 12:1–2).

Over the years, I have had a few people take a similar attitude in our church. My responsibility is to keep order in the services. I try to operate in love and protect the congregation. I have had a few people stand up in the middle of a service and give a revelation that is totally out of order. When I asked them to sit down and wait, they got mad and stormed out, saying, "Is he the only one who knows how to move in the Holy Spirit?" That is an ugly attitude, and it is not biblical.

You will never grow in the Lord if you do not respect the leadership God sets over a congregation. Any revelation from God can be held in your spirit until the right time to give it. I have held a prophecy in my spirit for a day or two. You may think, *God gave it to me, and I cannot control it.* If you cannot control it, it is not of God.

The Bible says that when Miriam and Aaron spoke against Moses, God heard it. We never have a right to criticize anyone. Every child of God has an important function in the body of Christ. God sees His children differently than we see them. Notice what He said about Moses: "Not so with My servant Moses; he is faithful in all My house. I speak with him face to face, even plainly, and not in dark sayings; and he sees the form of the LORD. Why then were you not afraid to speak against My servant Moses?" (Numbers 12:7–8).

God had spoken to Moses face to face, and yet they were critical of him. Miriam and Aaron had also been chosen for great tasks. Why should they be jealous of Moses? They should have been glad for the ministry that God had given them.

Miriam and Aaron's critical and proud attitude provoked the anger of God, and Miriam was struck with leprosy. Moses interceded on her behalf, and God healed her, but the Israelites' journey was delayed for seven days. The whole move of God was stopped because two people had exaggerated opinions of their importance.

Miriam and Aaron's attitude cut them off from the abundance of God as well as their usefulness, until they repented. When God begins to use you in the gifts of the Holy Spirit, when He begins to bless you and give you revelations, let it humble you more and more. It is not you; it is God.

Be Little in Your Own Eyes

Consider the life of King Saul in the Old Testament. Saul was a fine-looking man. The Bible says that he was head and shoulders above all the rest of the men (1 Samuel 9:2). He was the first king over Israel, and God used him mightily. However, Saul disobeyed God and fell from favor with Him. The prophet Samuel interceded on Saul's behalf, but God rejected Saul as king. God spoke through Samuel and made a statement about Saul's attitude that we should always remember: "When you were little in your own eyes, were you not head of the tribes of Israel? And did not the LORD anoint you king over Israel?" (1 Samuel 15:17).

When you were little in your own eyes is the secret. When we are little in our own eyes, God is pleased with us because we know that we can do nothing without Him. If we will have a low estimation of our own importance, God will use us. After all, "Pride goes before destruction, and a haughty spirit before a fall" (Proverbs 16:18), and "Before destruction the heart of a man is haughty, and before honor is humility" (Proverbs 18:12).

Let your confession be what you have in Christ and not what you can do in your own power and ability.

HUMBLE YOURSELF UNDER GOD'S MIGHTY HAND

Search the Scriptures and read biographies, and you discover that many great men and women of God have spent years doing insignificant tasks that God asked them to do. The Bible encourages us to not despise the day of small beginnings (Zechariah 4:10). When you prove yourself faithful to God in the little things, He will trust you with much. "He who is faithful in what is least is faithful also in much; and he who is unjust in what is least is unjust also in much" (Luke 16:10).

In the book of Acts, the number of disciples increased, and there arose a problem with serving tables and the distribution of clothing and food. The apostles felt that they should give themselves continually to prayer and the preaching of the Word of God; therefore, they appointed seven men to handle the food and clothing. "Then the twelve summoned the multitude of the disciples and said, 'It is not desirable that we should leave the word of God and serve tables. Therefore, brethren, seek out from among you seven men of good reputation, full of the Holy Spirit and wisdom, whom we may appoint over this business'" (Acts 6:2–3).

These seven men were not just ordinary men. The Bible states they were full of the Holy Spirit and wisdom. They were powerful men, and yet they were chosen to serve tables and distribute clothing. These men could have said, "Look, I am not called to serve tables. God called me to preach." They could have had an exaggerated opinion of their importance, but they were faithful to do what needed to be done.

God will bless people who are willing to take a lower position in the eyes of men. He will exalt the humble. "Therefore humble yourselves under the mighty hand of God, that He may exalt you in due time" (1 Peter 5:6).

It was not long before one of the seven men began to shine. Stephen became a powerful preacher, who did great wonders and miracles among the people. The Bible says that no one was able to resist the wisdom and the Spirit by which he spoke (Acts 6:8–10). Soon Stephen was arrested and taken to the Jewish council, but everyone who looked at him saw that his face was shining like the face of an angel.

God will exalt the humble.

The power of God in Stephen's life provoked the anger of his enemies, and they dragged him out of the city and stoned him to death. The heavens were opened, and Stephen saw the glory of God. "But he, being full of the Holy Spirit, gazed into heaven and saw the glory of God, and Jesus standing at the right hand of God, and said, 'Look! I see the heavens opened and the Son of Man standing at the right hand of God!'" (Acts 7:55–56).

The person who lives a life of humility is the person who will walk in the supernatural power of God.

Stephen said he saw Jesus *standing* at the right hand of God, yet we are told repeatedly in Scripture that Jesus is *seated* at the right hand of the Father. I believe that Jesus thought, *In honor to Stephen, I will stand to receive his spirit. I will stand for a man who was faithful to serve tables. I will stand for a man who will give his life for the sake of the Gospel.*

God honors men and women who will do humble tasks for Him.

Philip was another disciple who waited on the tables. He began to preach in Samaria, and the whole city was stirred by miracles, signs, and wonders (Acts 8:6–8). An angel of God appeared to Philip and sent him to the desert to lead an Ethiopian man to the Lord. After baptizing this man, Philip was supernaturally translated to the city of Azotus, where he began preaching.

This is what happens to the person who will walk humbly before the Lord. The person who lives a life of humility is the person who will walk in the supernatural power of God.

Let there be no fighting over the high positions. Give unqualified courtesy and respect to every person. Serve one another in love. Walk humbly before God, and you will be blessed with riches, honor, and life.

We reign in life as kings and walk in the abundance of God through the power of humility.

We reign in life as kings by One, Christ Jesus, who "humbled Himself and became obedient to the point of death, even the death on the cross" (Philippians 2:8). Let us follow His example.

Reflections from JOEL

Some people live in despair and disappointment, all because their circumstances are not exactly what they desire them to be. They are never happy unless everything is going their way, everybody is treating them right, and they are immune from experiencing discomfort. In other words, they never are happy! That's a very shallow way to live.

Certainly, none of us enjoy going through struggles, but you have to understand that your struggle may be an opportunity for advancement and promotion. The very thing you are fighting against so tenaciously may be the springboard that catapults you to a new level of excellence. Your challenges may become your greatest assets.

Without the resistance of air, an eagle can't soar. Without the resistance of water, a ship can't float. Without the resistance of gravity, you and I can't even walk. Without opposition or resistance, there is no potential for progress. There are no shortcuts; there's no easy way to mature physically, emotionally, or spiritually. You must remain determined and walk humbly with God. Salvation is more than a onetime prayer. It is constantly cooperating with God, dealing with the issues He brings up, keeping a humble attitude, and allowing Him to change you as He sees fit.

CHAPTER EIGHT

An Abundance
of the
Holy Spirit
for Changing
the World

In the Introduction, I began to teach about the work of the Holy Spirit in our lives. It is, unfortunately, one of the most neglected teachings of the church and is the primary reason that there is so little of the abundance of God and His power in today's church.

Luke, in writing the Acts of the Apostles, begins: "And being assembled together with them, [Jesus] commanded them not to depart from Jerusalem, but to wait for the Promise of the Father, 'which,' He said, 'you have heard from Me; for John truly baptized with water, but you shall be baptized with the Holy Spirit not many days from now. . . . But you shall receive power when the Holy Spirit has come upon you; and you shall be witnesses to Me in Jerusalem, and in all Judea and Samaria, and to the end of the earth'" (Acts 1:4–5, 8).

The book of Acts is a picture of the New Testament church, the body of Christ. It has been called by many names, but God started just one church. This is not a denomination. It is not the beginning of a church that has changed. All believers bear one Name, and that is the Name of Jesus. All people who put their faith in Jesus and have received His Holy Spirit are in the body of Christ, regardless of whatever denomination they have chosen.

The book of Acts is a pattern for the church in every century. Every generation should produce similar acts within the body of Christ. We should continue the record of the book of Acts by doing the same things! The epistles are the instructions for the church, but the primary pattern in the book of Acts is our example for today.

What the Holy Spirit Does

God wrote the Bible for every person. Every believer in every denomination has a right to know what God has given them as members of His church. None are to be denied the power of the Living God in this dark generation in which we are living. All God's children have a right to know and experience God's power.

Jesus spoke in the first chapter of Acts about the power of the Holy Spirit. We need to believe what the Lord Jesus says. Do not make void the Word and commandment of God by what your religious tradition says. God is wanting to pour out a mighty revival of the power of the Lord Jesus that restores the church to what it has lost through the centuries.

Jesus spoke clearly about being born of the Spirit. He said, "Most assuredly, I say to you, unless one is born of water and the Spirit, he cannot enter the kingdom of God" (John 3:5).

Jesus also talked as clearly about being baptized in the Holy Spirit, about receiving the power of God, in the verses I quoted previously. When He said, "You shall be baptized with the Holy Spirit," He was not stating a doctrine for any particular denomination. This is simply a Christian doctrine, a command of Jesus, who is the Supreme Head of the church.

Just because we are born of the Spirit in salvation does not mean we do not need Jesus to baptize us in the Holy Spirit. Just because you get a "well" of salvation does not mean that you do not need to be baptized by the Lord Jesus Christ and have "rivers of living water" flowing out of you to a needy world (John 4:14; 7:38).

In salvation, the Holy Spirit does something to you. He regenerates your spirit and makes you a new creation. Every believer in Jesus has the presence of the Holy Spirit in their spirit. "Now if anyone does not have the Spirit of Christ, he is not His" (Romans 8:9). Every believer has the Holy Spirit witnessing with his spirit that he is a child of God (Romans 8:16).

In the baptism of the Holy Spirit, Jesus does something to you. John the Baptist declared, "I indeed baptize you with water unto repentance, but He who is coming after me is mightier than I, whose sandals I am not worthy to carry. He will baptize you with the Holy Spirit and fire" (Matthew 3:11). You should not be afraid of what Jesus will do to you or for you.

Continual Power From God

This is an hour when we need to tell people what Jesus has to say. In Acts 1:1, it tells "of all that Jesus began both to do and teach." I am so glad Jesus did not finish everything in the Gospels. Of course, He finished the work of redemption through the cross and resurrection. But we are to continue to carry on the work of the church as started in the book of Acts.

Jesus "commanded" the apostles that they were "not to depart from Jerusalem, but to wait for the Promise of the Father" (Acts 1:4). The command from Jesus was to wait. They had not yet received the power of the Holy Spirit.

Many church people love the Lord Jesus. They are doing the best they know how to do to serve Him. They are walking in all the light they have, but they do not know what Jesus commanded them! They need to take off their religious glasses and unplug their denominational headphones, then read the Bible and simply believe what it says. Do not just let another person tell you what they think the Bible is saying. Read it for yourself.

All God's children
have a right to know and experience
GOD'S POWER.

Jesus commanded the disciples to not leave Jerusalem until they had received power from on high. He told them they were not ready to be His witnesses without that power of the Holy Spirit. He said, "But you shall receive power when the Holy Spirit has come upon you; and you shall be witnesses to Me in Jerusalem, and in all Judea and Samaria, and to the end of the earth" (Acts 1:8).

I do not know of anyone who is making a living, raising a family, and trying to serve God who does not need the ability, efficiency, and might of the Holy Spirit. Jesus said, "You shall receive power." This power does not work just as *dynamite* to bring one explosive experience in your life. It is continual power from God! It works as a *dynamo* on the inside of you. It gives continual light and power throughout the years. "But the path of the just is like the shining sun, that shines ever brighter unto the perfect day" (Proverbs 4:18).

Jesus said we would receive power and be witnesses to Him wherever we go and whatever we do. We should go out with joy into our neighborhoods and into this hungering and thirsting generation with the good news about Jesus, who is the same yesterday, today, and forever!

DESPERATELY HUNGRY FOR GOD

I can remember when I had not received the baptism of the Holy Spirit. For nineteen years I pastored churches and did my very best. I knew the presence of God in a shallow way, but I did not have any continuing power. I had learned and accepted the fact that this was the way it was. I had been taught in college and seminary that all the supernatural work of the Holy Spirit had passed away with the last apostle. There were to be no more signs and no more miracles. "All supernatural things ended when the last apostle died," they said.

Think about that teaching for a moment. How ridiculous! Why would God do that? I was taught this sad thing, and I believed it.

I thank God that there are people in all churches today who are sick and tired of being sick and tired of this nonsense! They are weary of a form of godliness that denies the power! They are not going to be denied the power of God any longer! Hunger for the things of God is a wonderful thing. It will bring God on the scene.

John G. Lake, a preacher of another generation who shook nations for God, said, "Hunger can be a good thing. It is the greatest persuader I know of. It is a marvelous power. Nations have learned that you can do almost anything with a populace until they get hungry. But when they get hungry, watch out. There is a certain spirit of desperation that accompanies hunger."

I wish we all had it spiritually. I wish we were desperately hungry for God. Wouldn't it be glorious?

I will guarantee you that after the crucifixion and resurrection of Jesus there were 120 mighty hungry people in the upper room in Jerusalem. If they had not been exceedingly hungry, they would not have gotten so gloriously filled. It was because they were hungry that they were filled.

No matter what your soul may be desiring, *if God's power becomes the supreme cry of your life, not the secondary matter, or the third or tenth, but the supreme desire of your soul, the paramount issue—all the powers and energies of your spirit, soul, and body are reaching out and crying to God for the answer—it is going to come!*

Over the years, especially through what seemed to be a family cycle of constant sickness and disease, I finally got to the place where my supreme heart cry was for deliverance. I could hear the groans and cries and feel my family's desperation for wellness. My heart cried, my soul sobbed, my spirit wept tears. I wanted help. I did not know enough to call directly on God for it. (Isn't it a strange thing that we do not have enough sense to call on God for physical difficulties as well as spiritual ones? But I did not.)

If God's power becomes the supreme cry of your life, it is going to come!

But one thing matured in my heart—a real hunger. And the hunger of a man's soul must be satisfied. It is a law of God that is in the depths of the Spirit. God will answer the heart that cries; God will answer the soul that asks. Christ Jesus comes to us with divine assurance and invites us when we are hungry, to pray, to believe, to take from the Lord that for which our soul desires and our heart yearns.

One day the Lord of heaven came our way, and in a little while the cloud of darkness, that curse of death, was lifted. The light of God shone into our lives and into our home, just the same as it existed in other men's lives and other men's homes. We learned the truth of Jesus and were able to apply the divine power of God. We were healed of the Lord. "Blessed are those who hunger and thirst for righteousness, for they shall be filled" (Matthew 5:6).

God created a supernatural hunger and a thirst in my heart for more of Him. I began to feel a divine restlessness. There was a divine dissatisfaction in my spirit. I said, "Oh, God, I do not want to die without having had a more fruitful ministry. I want to see more than I have ever seen in all of my life." That was the beginning of my quest for the baptism in the Holy Spirit.

Rejoice if there has been an awakening in your heart for the same! Be glad that there is a hunger and thirst in your heart. Be glad that God smiled upon you to give you a desire to come to Him. Jesus said,

"If you then, being evil,

KNOW HOW TO GIVE GOOD GIFTS

to your children,

how much more will your Father

WHO IS IN HEAVEN

give good things to those who ask Him!"

(MATTHEW 7:11)

SUPERNATURAL POWER IS AVAILABLE

Another thing that brought me to the realization of the truth of the baptism of the Holy Spirit was the healing of our daughter Lisa. When she was born, my wife, who is a registered nurse, knew immediately that something was wrong. Our pediatrician confirmed it later. She told us that our baby had brain damage and would never be normal. She had no sucking reflexes, no muscle tone, and symptoms similar to cerebral palsy. She was not able to lift her head from the bed, even a fraction of an inch, until she was five months old, and she never had enough strength to crawl.

We needed a miracle! I had been a pastor for nineteen years, but I knew very little about healing. The books in my library and my seminary professors said God sent sickness to bless us or teach us good lessons. They said little about the miracle-working power of God.

I read the four Gospels until I began to see Jesus.

Desperate for an answer, I closed my office and went alone day after day with the Word of God. I read the four Gospels until I began to see Jesus. There emerged from those pages a mighty compassionate miracle worker. He was not the person I had been taught. He was the Son of the Living God who is the same yesterday, today, and forever!

I beheld Him as One greater than all our concepts of Him! I saw Him as One great and loving enough to encompass all people everywhere in His mighty arms! We read His promises to us over and over. We saw that it was not God's will that Lisa be afflicted, but rather that God wanted to heal her.

Those were some dark days for us as we struggled to believe. But God was so merciful and compassionate. Days turned into weeks, and weeks into months, as we stood fast on the promises of God to heal her. Then one glorious day, Jesus touched our baby. She was delivered!

I am sure the angels watching broke forth in a heavenly song, praising God for His love and faithfulness to His Word. I am sure our blessed Jesus smiled at our joy, for He had taken all our sins, sicknesses, and pains in His own body and purchased our healing. And today, Lisa remains every bit whole, a mighty miracle of God!

Now we knew that God's supernatural power was available in our day. *God's power is for today!*

The Power of Worship and Praise

Another thing that helped me receive the baptism of the Holy Spirit was the power in worship and praise that I witnessed among Spirit-filled believers. Although I felt out of place going to a Spirit-filled prayer meeting, I was desperately hungry for God's power. I remember the most remarkable thing happened there. The believers got down on their knees, lifted their hands to God, worshiped God, and prayed all at the same time. Next to me, there was a woman kneeling and worshiping the Lord. Tears streamed down her cheeks as she praised Him. There was an indefinable, indescribable beauty in her countenance that filled me with wonder.

I said to myself, "What is this? What does this woman have? What makes these tears come? What gives her the ability to enter into worship like this? What is this marvelous, wonderful ability to praise God that I don't have?" This profound experience was a turning point in my long search.

Never underestimate the power of the believer in praise and worship. A watching world needs the power of God. That experience in my life generated the power to go on in my quest for more of God. I never got away from that. That was what was missing in my life!

I wanted the fullness of the Holy Spirit in my life, and I did receive the baptism of the Holy Spirit! Now I daily enjoy this heavenly worship and supernatural language. It is so wonderful just to lift my hands and adore and worship the Lord.

Never be ashamed to lift your hands. Never be ashamed to let your praises rise to heaven. It has a powerful effect on others as well as blessing and pleasing our Father God.

I believe there is a coming day when God's people, filled with the Holy Spirit, will fill the streets of our cities in multitudes. They will lift their hands and praise God and boldly declare the Good News of salvation. They will pray for the sick and cast out demons. They will shake the cities of the nations by the power of the Holy Spirit!

NEVER UNDERESTIMATE

the power

OF THE BELIEVER

in praise and worship.

Reflections from
JOEL

*T*he apostle Paul tells us to "be filled with the Spirit, speaking to one another in psalms and hymns and spiritual songs, singing and making melody in your heart to the Lord" (Ephesians 5:18–19). This is to be the norm, not the exception, to how we live.

It's not always easy to stay excited and inspired. Perhaps at one time you were deeply in love, full of passion, but now your marriage has become stale and stagnant. Or maybe you were excited about your job, but it's become dull and boring. Maybe at one time you were excited about serving God. You couldn't wait to get to church. You loved reading your Bible, praying, and spending time with fellow believers. But lately you've been thinking, "I don't know what's wrong with me. I don't have any passion. I'm just going through the motions."

The truth is, much of life is routine, and we can become stagnant if we're not careful to stay filled with the Holy Spirit. He alone can renew our spirit daily.

CHAPTER NINE

An Abundance *of* Freedom for Every Stronghold

When I finally received the baptism of the Holy Spirit, I was like Jonah in the belly of the great fish. I was still inside of my denomination, just as Jonah was inside of that fish, and the fish was saying, "I am going to digest and absorb you." Old Jonah began to kick and fight and said, "You will not digest me with those gastric juices. I am getting out!" Then the fish got a terrible stomachache and got rid of Jonah!

My denomination said, "Whatever you say you have experienced will pass over. We will digest you with our denominational gastric juices and get the baptism of the Holy Spirit out of you." But when I got through kicking and fighting, they got rid of me!

This is the day when God is getting people to hear one Name, the Name of the Lord Jesus Christ. People are arising who put Jesus and their allegiance to Him and the glorious power of the Holy Spirit above everything else in the world.

Acts 2:1 states, "When the Day of Pentecost had fully come . . ." Let the Day of Pentecost come. Let it come in love, joy, peace, longsuffering, gentleness, goodness, faith, meekness, and self-control (Galatians 5:22–23). We should have the full power of love. Let it fully come in the power of the gifts of the Holy Spirit.

The Release of Your Spirit

"When the Day of Pentecost had fully come, they were all with one accord in one place. And suddenly there came a sound from heaven, as of a rushing mighty wind, and it filled the whole house where they were sitting. Then there appeared to them divided tongues, as of fire, and one sat upon each of them. And they were all filled with the Holy Spirit and began to speak with other tongues, as the Spirit gave them utterance" (Acts 2:1–4).

This is an account of the release of the spirit of man. It is the flow of spiritual freedom for man's reborn spirit!

You are a spirit. You have a soul. You live in a body. Your spirit was dead to God. When Adam sinned, his light went out—the light of his spirit vanished. When Eve sinned, the light of her spirit went out. Life left them, and death came to them spiritually.

"And you He made alive, who were dead in trespasses and sins, in which you once walked according to the course of this world, according to the prince of the power of the air, the spirit who now works in the sons of disobedience, among whom also we all once conducted ourselves in the lusts of our flesh, fulfilling the desires of the flesh and of the mind, and were by nature children of wrath, just as the others" (Ephesians 2:1–3).

When you came into this world, you were dead to God in your spirit. There are only two kinds of people in this world: children of God and children of the devil (1 John 3:10). Either God is your Father or the devil is your father (John 8:42–44). You are motivated either by God or the devil. Every lost person has the devil as his father (Ephesians 2:2).

The person who is a child of the devil has spiritual death residing on the inside of him. The person who is a child of God is a spirit that has eternal life. God is his Father. When you receive Jesus Christ, God imparts His eternal life into your spirit through the Holy Spirit.

However, we can be born again and have God's life in us and not have that spirit free. The baptism of the Holy Spirit sets you free in your spirit!

Spiritually Alive but Still Bound

Let me illustrate this spiritual principle through the story of Lazarus (John 11). Lazarus was dead, yet Jesus told the people that if they would believe, they would see the glory of God. Jesus wept as He came to the grave, and then He cried out, "Lazarus, come forth!"

Lazarus came forth and received life. He came out, but he was bound with grave clothes around his body and a napkin was about his mouth. He was bound! He was alive, but he was not free!

Multitudes of believers in all denominations have received eternal life, but they are still bound in religious grave clothes. Jesus said, "Loose Lazarus, and let him go!" and He's saying the same to His church today: "Loose them, and let them go!"

Jesus wants us free
so we can go in the power of the Holy Spirit and evangelize the world!

When I accepted Jesus Christ as my Savior, I was truly saved. I had spiritual life, but I was not free. I needed the freedom to live and act like the Christians in the book of Acts. I needed to be free to praise God. I needed the religious napkin taken off my mouth to be able to worship God in spirit and in truth.

Earlier in the book, I wrote about the little bird that was hatched in a cage and never knew there was anything more than the cage in which it was confined. Then one day the cage door was left open, and it flew out and through the window—set free to fly as it was meant to fly. That little bird represents my story. I was hatched in my religious birdcage, and there I sat on my swing. I ate my religious birdseed and sang my religious songs. Thank God, I finally got out to enjoy all the free blessings and abundance of God.

You do not have to leave your church—just get set free! Be free to live and walk in the Holy Spirit. Love all of God's people. It is all right to be in your church as long as you are not being restricted from being full of the Holy Spirit.

Enter Into the Realm of the Supernatural

When you receive the baptism of the Holy Spirit, there is a release in your spirit, and that spirit man begins to be active. The first thing that spirit man begins to do is talk. On the day of Pentecost, the believers began to speak in other languages, which was the release of their spirits.

Think about meeting God face to face and never having had the privilege of your spirit man talking to Him before. Whenever we talk by the Holy Spirit, we are talking beyond the ability of our mind to comprehend. "For he who speaks in a tongue does not speak to men but to God, for no one understands him; however, in the spirit he speaks mysteries. . . . For if I pray in a tongue, my spirit prays, but my understanding is unfruitful" (1 Corinthians 14:2, 14).

That is the release of your spirit!

You should let yourself talk to God every day by your spirit energized by the Holy Spirit. "But the hour is coming, and now is, when the true worshipers will worship the Father in spirit and truth; for the Father is seeking such to worship Him. God is Spirit, and those who worship Him must worship in spirit and truth" (John 4:23–24).

God the Father is seeking His children to worship Him in spirit and in truth. By worshiping Him in the Spirit, He is referring to speaking to Him in a spiritual language.

You may wonder if you have to speak in tongues when you receive the baptism of the Holy Spirit. Look at this way: you get to speak in another language! It is a sign that you have received the fullness of the Holy Spirit.

When you begin to speak in other tongues, your spirit man is released. The joy of praying to the Father, of bypassing your mind and going directly to the throne of God, speaking in a spiritual language, is wonderful. No one should be denied their right to be released in their spirit.

When you are released in your spirit, God puts you into a spiritual dimension beyond anything you have ever known. Through the Holy Spirit, you touch a realm you never before touched, even in your deepest dedication. It is a dimension where the gifts of the Holy Spirit operate. It is the realm of the supernatural! You begin to live in the same Holy Spirit-charged atmosphere as those in the book of Acts.

The release of the spirit enables you to walk in the realm of the gifts of the Holy Spirit. *The Amplified Bible* states that the supernatural gifts are "the special endowments of supernatural energy" (1 Corinthians 12:1). According to 1 Corinthians 12:4–10, there is . . .

> *the gift of miracles,*
> *the gift of faith,*
> *the gift of healing,*
> *the gift of tongues,*
> *the gift of interpretation of tongues,*
> *the gift of prophecy,*
> *the gift of the word of wisdom,*
> *the gift of the word of knowledge,*
> *and the gift of discerning of spirits.*

Thank God, these are the weapons of our spiritual warfare, given to us by the Holy Spirit.

Oh, I wish I could fully tell you the joy and blessings of the mighty baptism of the Holy Spirit! Let me urge you to seek the Lord Jesus for this outpouring of power!

That longing inside of you is for this power of God. Your spirit is yearning to be released—to communicate with your heavenly Father in the deepest fashion. God loves you so much! He sees your desire for freedom and power. He knows you belong to Him. You need to do more than swing in your religious swing and eat your religious birdseed.

The door is wide open!

Come forth and join multitudes of your other brothers and sisters in the family of God who are enjoying the abundant blessings of our heavenly Father.

Your spirit needs this release to talk and to live in the realm of the supernatural. So much can happen when your spirit is set free. When your spirit is liberated, you receive the ability to act like a spirit person and live as a spirit person, and not just as a soulish, physical person.

FEED YOUR SPIRIT WITH SPIRITUAL FOOD

Jesus said, "It is the Spirit who gives life; the flesh profits nothing. The words that I speak to you are spirit, and they are life" (John 6:63). A physical man must have physical food. A spirit man must have spiritual food.

Jesus said His words are life: "Man shall not live by bread alone, but by every word that proceeds from the mouth of God" (Matthew 4:4). As you are released in the spirit to talk in a heavenly language and walk in the gifts of the Holy Spirit, you must realize that you are released to go to the table of God and feed on spiritual food. You need to read and feed upon the Word of God!

Many believers feed their bodies three good meals a day and their spirit one cold snack a week! Then they wonder why they are not growing spiritually! If you will feed your spirit as much as you feed your body, you will be a healthy Christian.

You have victory in the realm where you feed! Do not continue to feed your carnal nature on the things of this world. Some people know every football player, every fishing lure and reel, every hunting gun and shells, and everything they need to know to indulge and feed their soul (mind, will, and emotions), yet they hardly know an apostle from an epistle!

Start feeding that spirit man on spiritual food. Talk as a spirit man in the spirit language. Walk in the realm of the gifts of the Holy Spirit. Feed your spirit on the Word of God, while starving your carnal nature.

You will be a strong spiritual person. You will be victorious in every battle and over every stronghold!

Release your spirit to flow in the fullness of God! You will be used of God as you flow in the freedom of the Spirit!

Reflections from
JOEL

Some people are outgoing and energetic; others are more timid and laid-back. Some people like to wear suits and ties; other people are more comfortable wearing blue jeans. Some people close their eyes and lift their hands when they worship God; others worship God in a more subdued manner. And God likes it all!

Don't think that you have to fit into somebody else's mold. You were not created to mimic somebody else. God doesn't want a bunch of clones. He likes variety, and you should not let people pressure you or make you feel badly about yourself because you don't fit their image of who you should be. You don't need anybody else's approval. God has given us all different gifts, talents, and personalities on purpose. When you go around trying to be like somebody else, not only does it demean you, it steals your uniqueness.

Be an original, not a copycat. Dare to be different; be secure in who God made you to be and then go out and be the best you that you can be. Ask God to fill you with the power of the Holy Spirit. The Holy Spirit will help you run your race and be the best that you can be.

CHAPTER TEN

An Abundance *of* Miracles *for* Your Impossibilities

The book of Acts sets the pattern for the New Testament church. Everyone who is born of the Spirit is in the family of God. I see a tremendous spiritual hunger today in the hearts of all of God's people in all denominations. There is not a wall strong enough or high enough to keep them away from the power of the Holy Spirit. They are going to be filled with God's holy power!

AN ABUNDANCE OF MIRACLES FOR YOUR IMPOSSIBILITIES | 203

If you want to know what God started, read the book of Acts. If it does not agree with your religious doctrine, put aside your doctrine and believe the Bible.

Acts 1 gives the promise of God to baptize His people with the Holy Spirit and power. Acts 2 tells of the release of your spirit when you receive the baptism of the Holy Spirit and speak in tongues. Acts 3 tells us that as soon as they were clothed with power, as soon as they had a release in their spirits, immediately this New Testament church saw the flow of the supernatural power of God.

"Now Peter and John went up together to the temple at the hour of prayer, the ninth hour. And a certain man lame from his mother's womb was carried, whom they laid daily at the gate of the temple which is called Beautiful, to ask alms from those who entered the temple; who, seeing Peter and John about to go into the temple, asked for alms. And fixing his eyes on him, with John, Peter said, 'Look at us.' So he gave them his attention, expecting to receive something from them" (Acts 3:1–5).

Thank God that when you look on someone who is full of the Holy Spirit, expecting to receive something from them, you *can* receive it! The lame man was full of expectation! He may not have expected what he received, but he expected.

"Then Peter said, 'Silver and gold I do not have, but what I do have I give you: In the name of Jesus Christ of Nazareth, rise up and walk.' And he took him by the right hand and lifted him up, and immediately his feet and ankle bones received strength. So he, leaping up, stood and walked and entered the temple with them—walking, leaping, and praising God" (Acts 3:6–8).

You must realize that you are not prepared to touch the world effectively until you are empowered by God through the baptism of the Holy Spirit.

The baptism of the Holy Spirit is a doorway into a way of life!

This is not the goal. It is a doorway into a way of life! It is an entrance into the supernatural gifts of the Holy Spirit.

Some people have the idea that when they receive the baptism of the Holy Spirit they can just sit down and that is all there is to it. No! It is the beginning of a glorious supernatural life where there is no end to helping needy humanity find salvation, healing, and help through the Lord Jesus Christ.

The Gifts of the Spirit Are for Every Believer

God wants every man, every woman, and every child to be filled with the Holy Spirit and move on in the gifts, power, and energy of the Holy Spirit!

Consider the following three passages of Scripture from the *Amplified Bible*:

The spiritual gifts of the Holy Spirit are "the special endowments of supernatural energy" (1 Corinthians 12:1).

"Now there are distinctive varieties and distributions of endowments (gifts, extraordinary powers distinguishing certain Christians, due to the power of divine grace operating in their souls by the Holy Spirit) and they vary, but the [Holy] Spirit remains the same" (1 Corinthians 12:4).

"But to each one is given the manifestation of the [Holy] Spirit [the evidence, the spiritual illumination of the Spirit] for good and profit" (1 Corinthians 12:7).

You see, the spiritual gifts are special endowments of supernatural energy! They are extraordinary powers that distinguish Christians. Every person receives this manifestation of the Holy Spirit, this spiritual illumination.

As soon as the early church received the baptism of the Holy Spirit, immediately the supernatural began to radiate and emanate from their lives! They began to do the works that Jesus did as He had promised (John 14:12).

You do not have to be an apostle, pastor, or elder to flow in God's power. Every believer has this same miraculous power available to him.

The Bible says, "And these signs will follow those who believe: In My name they will cast out demons; they will speak with new tongues; they will take up serpents; and if they drink anything deadly, it will by no means hurt them; they will lay hands on the sick, and they will recover" (Mark 16:17–18).

Jesus left us a pattern for the church today. As soon as these believers were filled with the Holy Spirit, immediately the supernatural began to flow.

There are thousands of people who are held in bondage by the enemy's power because they have been denied the supernatural power of God. Their hearts cry out for the supernatural. When we deny them the true power of God, they go to the false supernatural—the occult and witchcraft.

Today there is arising an army of God's people clothed with God's power that will show this generation the true way to supernatural power. Every child of God should be a channel of the supernatural energy and the divine gifts of the Holy Spirit.

If the spiritual gifts are not operating in your life, you should stir yourself to pray and seek God. The gifts of the Spirit are the weapons of our warfare. "For the weapons of our warfare are not carnal but mighty in God for pulling down strongholds" (2 Corinthians 10:4).

We are endowed with these gifts that we might fight the good fight of faith and deliver our generation (1 Timothy 6:12). There is no greater thrill than to see God work through your human flesh! It is the most wonderful experience in the world!

Declare the Word of God

When I first received the baptism of the Holy Spirit, I wanted everything that God would give me. I was so thrilled to find out the truth about the gifts of the Holy Spirit. As I began my ministry, I would pray for the gifts of the Spirit. I wanted all nine of them to operate in my life. Somehow, in all my sincerity but also in all my ignorance, I expected a little angel to come down and touch me. From then on, I would have these gifts. Sparks would fly as the angel touched me, and I would be endowed with these wonderful gifts from God!

I didn't know any better.

As I sought God, He told me to go out and stand before sighing, crying, dying humanity and preach the Word, and He would be there with me. He would confirm the Word with signs following in a flow of the supernatural.

So I decided to have a meeting and rented an auditorium. I was so excited as hundreds of people came. I told them my background and what God had done in my life by His Spirit. I told them that Jesus was the same yesterday, today, and forever (Hebrews 13:8). I told them that God has given us the power to cast out demons, to lay hands on the sick and see them healed (Mark 16:17–18). I told them that they would see miracles in Jesus' Name.

People began to line up for prayer. I was astonished! People had believed the Word of God that I preached!

I quieted my spirit before the people. The first person who marched across the stage was a mute man. He had never spoken a word in all his life! I thought to myself, *Oh, God, couldn't I start with someone with a stomachache?* Of course, this was only a natural thought. The same power that could heal a stomachache could heal this man.

Thank God for the anointing of the Holy Spirit! As I stood there with butterflies in my stomach, I was reminded of the great promises of God.

I did not feel like it, but I acted like God had told me the truth in His Word. Jesus had promised me, "Behold, I give you the authority to trample on serpents and scorpions, and over all the power of the enemy, and nothing shall by any means hurt you" (Luke 10:19).

I prayed for that man in the Name of the Lord Jesus Christ. He could hear, but he could not talk. So I put the microphone by his mouth, and I told him to say, "Thank you, Jesus!" He did, and the meeting was on!

In that meeting, we saw such miracles of God, such mighty demonstrations of salvation, divine healing, and deliverance. It was a marvelous thing to behold as Jesus met the needs of the people!

Live in the Power of the Holy Spirit

You do not have to feel like God's power is in you. Believe God. You have the Holy Spirit. Go in the Name of Jesus! God expects you to live and move in the power of the Holy Spirit.

The Bible says that the gifts of the Holy Spirit are divided to every man, woman, and child as God wills. The manifestation of the gifts is for everyone. There is a divine gift that should be flowing in your life—*in your life!* You have not been left out. You can move in the mighty stream of the supernatural power of God.

It is so thrilling! It is so wonderful to see God work!

Begin to be concerned about humanity. Lay hands on people and minister to people in love. God will begin to manifest what He desires through your life.

If we are the New Testament church, we not only believe in salvation by grace, but we believe in the baptism of the Holy Spirit that clothes us with power.

It is not enough for us to be gathered together and sing and praise and laugh and rejoice. We must teach the Word of God and feed God's people. As they grow, they will be so filled with God's glory and God's truth that they will arise. They will go forth and begin to minister to people's needs in God's power. The lost will turn to Jesus and be saved.

You are on a dead-end street if you do not see that after you are clothed with power and speak in tongues, you have just entered into the doorway to a life of the supernatural. This is not just for preachers, but there is power for all of the body of Christ.

THERE IS A DIVINE GIFT
that should be flowing in your life!

The Flow of the Miraculous

It is thrilling to see God move supernaturally. I recall preaching in a small country church and recounting the marvelous deliverances of Jesus recorded in Mark 5. Just as I ended that message and closed my Bible, a woman slowly got up and approached me with her crutches. In her own words, Clara Neil McWhirter recounts her own story of the wonderful miracle of God:

In 1954, I had rheumatoid arthritis and lupus, which the doctors diagnosed that there was no cure for either one. I was in severe pain, could not move, and was in bed for three years. The pain was so great I could not stand to be touched. I had to be turned with a sheet and would take several hot baths a day to help relieve some of the pain. I had seven surgeries during this time.

After a time, I was able to get out of bed, but by 1963 I was so crippled I was confined to a wheelchair. I had a big knot on my neck that prevented me from turning my head and spurs on my heels and crooked fingers and toes. My body would swell so badly at times that I would look twice my weight, which was only 100 pounds.

In 1968, my dear husband became ill with tuberculosis. The doctor said that since I was a nurse, he would consent to my taking my husband home if we would go into strict isolation. So my husband and I and Jesus were confined to our four-room house for eighteen months. No one could come in, and we could not go out. But we were happy. I crawled from room to room, day and night, caring for him. Finally, he recovered, and we got out of isolation.

However, in just a few months he was diagnosed with cancer of the colon. I prayed and cared for him again for two and a half years, then in 1973, he went to be with Jesus.

Through twenty-one years of pain, I never knew what it was not to hurt. I had been in a wheelchair for twelve years. But one week before Pastor Osteen came to my daughter's church, I had a dream that I was walking down the aisle in a church without my crutches. I was speaking words I did not understand.

I went to church with my daughter, and Pastor Osteen preached the most beautiful sermon about Jesus' healing power and love and mercy. Just as the sermon ended, a sweet voice spoke in my ear, "Go now." My daughter was sitting next to me, but she hadn't said anything. I knew it was Jesus speaking to me.

I picked up my crutches and made my way to Pastor Osteen. I poured my heart out to him. Then he raised his right hand and with his index finger, he gently touched me on the forehead. As he did this, it was as though a bolt of lightning went throughout my entire body. My arms were drawn above my head by a great force. (My arms had not been above my shoulders for twelve years because of the pain.) My crutches gently fell to the ground as though carried by angels.

Jesus healed me instantly.

Every spur in every part my body—my heels and my spine—and even the big knot on the back of my neck that had prevented me from turning my head instantly disappeared!

Pastor Osteen put the microphone to my mouth and asked me if I had anything to say. Then the most beautiful language poured out of my mouth. Jesus had baptized me with the Holy Spirit, and I spoke with tongues, praising and magnifying Jesus, my Healer!

I returned to the doctor, and he confirmed that I was totally healed. Even the lupus was gone in a moment of time.

Two weeks after I was healed, I traveled through six states, over 6,000 miles, telling of the wonderful miracles that God had performed in my life.

This is but one story among hundreds of the flow of the miraculous. This is the move of the Holy Spirit!

You are not to receive the baptism of the Holy Spirit, speak a few words in another language, and say, "Well, I have it all. That is all there is to it." No! No! No!

The fullness of the Holy Spirit is a doorway into the flow of the miraculous power of God.

Isaiah 8:18 states, "Here am I and the children whom the LORD has given me! We are for signs and wonders in Israel from the LORD of hosts, who dwells in Mount Zion."

Let me encourage you to enter into the full flow of God's divine power!

It is not enough

FOR US TO BE GATHERED TOGETHER

AND SING AND PRAISE

AND LAUGH AND REJOICE.

Reflections from
JOEL

*T*he Scripture teaches that we shouldn't look at the things that are seen but at the things that are not seen; for the things that are seen are only temporary, but the things that are seen through our eyes of faith are eternal (2 Corinthians 4:18). One translation says, "The things that are seen are subject to change." That means your health or finances may not look too good today, but that's subject to change. Nothing may be going right in your life, but it's all subject to change.

If you want to see God restore what's been stolen from you, get up each morning expecting good things to happen. You need to know that in a moment of time, God could turn it all around. Suddenly you could get your miracle. Suddenly God could bring someone new into your life. Suddenly you could get that promotion. All it takes is one "suddenly." In a split second, with one touch of God's favor, everything can change.

Put your faith out there and remind yourself that God wants to restore good things back to you. Our attitude should be, I'm not going to sit around mourning over what I've lost. I may have been knocked down, but I'm going to get back up again in victory. I am going to walk in the power of the Holy Spirit and reach out to help others!

A Prayer
for the
Abundant Life

Perhaps as you've been reading this book, you've discovered that the reason you're not living in the abundance of God is because you've never had a personal relationship with God. If you're not walking with God, you'll never understand His will and all of His provisions for your life. But you can change that.

Jesus said, "I am the way, the truth, and the life. No one comes to the Father except through Me" (John 14:6). If you have never received Jesus Christ into your life as Lord and Savior, this is your moment. He has done all that is necessary for you to become His child. In order to complete that desire, all that is necessary, is a prayer.

"Dear God,

I admit that I am a sinner in need of Your help.

I ask you to forgive me of all my sin.

Jesus, I believe You are the Son of God,

and You died for my sins and

rose from the dead.

I invite You to come into my life and be my

Lord and Savior.

Help me to live in a way that pleases and honors

You. God, I thank You that You are now

> *my heavenly Father and I am Your child,*

> *and that You have a plan for my life.*

I want all that You have for me,

> *and I ask You to baptize me in Your*

> *Holy Spirit to help me live an abundant life.*

I want Your supernatural power to touch others.

I pray in Jesus' Name.

Amen."

It is so wonderful

TO SEE GOD WORK!